Preface

Hernani is a significant 19th century French play of major historical import. When thinking of *Hernani* and its impact on French theatre and society, I think of Wells' *Citizen Kane*, Coppolla's *Apocalypse Now*, Scorcese's *Taxi Driver*, and (arguably) De Palma's *Scarface* … it's just that kind of play.

On his way to authoring *Les Miserables*, the staging of Hernani in 1830 unclogged a French Theatre constipated by Classicists like Racine. Using common terms like *mouchoire* (handkerchief), Hugo and his loud horde of Romantics terrorized the Classicists. Fights broke out at performances as the audience polarized between the young Hugo and the old guard of French theatre. *La Bataille d'Hernani* on the 25th of February, 1830 is still studied in drama, theatre, and French literature programs worldwide.

I translated *Hernani* in 1979 as part of a special project at the University of California at San Diego under the direction of Dr. Jonathan Saville, who retired as a professor emeritus at UCSD and was a longtime theatre/arts critic for the *San Diego Reader*. Having just returned from a year abroad studying at the Faculté des Lettres in Poitiers, France, I needed a challenge. Dr. Saville was kind enough to oblige me. I continued to refine the draft into the 1980's.

Hernani

This translation has been used by students and faculty at many schools, including the University of Chicago, Oakland University, Colgate, University of Georgia, University of Utah, University of Windsor, Lawrence University, University of Ottawa, University of Alberta, Rollins College, Mount Holyoke, University of Saskatchewan and others. In June 2004, I was proud to find out the translation was used by the English National Opera as a reference for their production of Verdi's opera, *Ernani*.

Enjoy.

Copyright © 2003 by Pierre Bedard

ISBN 978-1-60530-827-2

ISBN 978-1-60530-827-2

90000>

9 781605 308272

Act I, Scene 1

> Enter **DONA JOSEFA**. A **KNOCK**
> sounds at a hidden door. A second
> **KNOCK** sounds.

DONA JOSEFA. Is it him? So soon?

> Another **KNOCK**.

He's knocking at the right door.

> Another **KNOCK**.

Quickly… I'll get it.

> Enter **DON CARLOS**.

Good day, brave knight. What? You're not Senor
Hernani! Guards! Help!

DON CARLOS. Two words more, maid, and
you die. Good day indeed. Is this the house of
Dona Sol, the niece and fiancée of the old Duke
of Pastrana? He's a good old man, good enough, it
seems, to be cheated. His niece receives a little
knight, every night. He couldn't force a mustache
on his face with makeup. This is where he comes,
right? Am I correct if I assume that this is the
place? Talk! Maybe you'll answer if I…

DONA JOSEFA. I thought two words would
spell my end.

DON CARLOS. All I want from you, maid, is
one word… yes… or no. Now tell me, is this the
home of Dona Sol?

DONA JOSEFA. Yes it is. Why do you ask?

DON CARLOS. For no reason. The duke, her future husband, is not here?

DONA JOSEFA. Don Ruy Gomez is not here.

DON CARLOS. She's waiting for the young one, right?

DONA JOSEFA. Yes. He should be here at any moment.

DON CARLOS. What luck!

DONA JOSEFA. Isn't it, though?

DON CARLOS. Enough woman! So it's here that they meet, right?

DONA JOSEFA. Yes.

DON CARLOS. Hide me somewhere.

DONA JOSEFA. You?

DON CARLOS. Of course. Who else?

DONA JOSEFA. Why?

DON CARLOS. Never mind why, hide me.

DONA JOSEFA. Me hide you?

DON CARLOS. Yes. Here.

DONA JOSEFA. Never.

> **DON CARLOS** pulls dagger and purse from his belt.

DON CARLOS. Please, maid, be kind enough to choose between this purse and dagger.

DONA JOSEFA. I'll take the purse.

DON CARLOS. An intelligent choice, maid.

> **DONA JOSEFA** opens cupboard door.

DONA JOSEFA. In here.

DON CARLOS. This coffin?

DONA JOSEFA. Like it or lump it.

DON CARLOS. I will. Is this where you keep your broom, witch?

> **DON CARLOS** enters cupboard.

DONA JOSEFA. A man! In here!

DON CARLOS. Am I so different from the young knight, maid?

DONA JOSEFA. Oh heavens, Dona Sol! Quick, shut the door!

> **DONA JOSEFA** closes cupboard door.

DON CARLOS. One more word from you, woman, and you die!

DONA JOSEFA. Oh my! Oh dear! Who is he? If only the master were home. Oh well, the other one should be here soon. This is his business, not mine. May the good Lord save us from a sure Hell. This could be worse, though. He could be a thief.

Act I, Scene 2

Enter **DONA SOL**.

DONA SOL. Josefa!

DONA JOSEFA. Madam?

DONA SOL. Oh! I fear some mishap. Hernani should be here. That must be him. Let him in before he knocks.

Enter **HERNANI**.

HERNANI. Dona Sol! Ah, finally, it's you. The voice that speaks to me is yours. Why does fate place my days so far away from yours? I need you desperately to help me forget all the others.

DONA SOL. My lord, your clothes are dripping. It must have rained hard.

HERNANI. If it did, I didn't notice.

DONA SOL. Take off your coat.

HERNANI. Dona Sol, my love, tell me. When at night you sleep, calm pure and innocent... when a happy slumber cracks your mouth and places its finger on your eyes, does an angel tell you how sweet you are to the forgotten one that all push aside and abandon?

DONA SOL. You are very late tonight, my lord. Tell me if you are cold.

HERNANI. I burn near you! Ah! When a jealous love boils in my head and a storm swells in my heart, what does it matter what cloud decides to throw down on me?

DONA SOL. Come now, give me your coat and the sword.

HERNANI. No. This is my other friend, innocent and true. Your uncle, Dona Sol, the old Duke, your future husband, is he here?

DONA SOL. No, he is not. This hour is ours.

HERNANI. This hour and that is all. For us, no more than an hour. After that, what does it matter? We must forget or die. Angel, an hour with you is worth a lifetime, an eternity.

DONA SOL. Hernani!

HERNANI. The old man's absence brings joy to my heart. Like a trembling thief, kicking down your door, I steal you for an hour and listen to your song, for only one hour. But I am happy, envied for losing my life for the theft of one hour.

DONA SOL. Calm yourself, Hernani. Josefa, please, go dry his coat.

Exit **DONA JOSEFA**.

Come here.

HERNANI. So, the Duke is not here?

DONA SOL. Oh! How big you are!

HERNANI. He is not here.

DONA SOL. Let's forget the Duke.

HERNANI. Think of him, Madam. You are to marry the old man. He loves you. Didn't he steal a kiss from you the other day? And you ask me not to think about him?

DONA SOL. Is that what's depressing you? An uncle's kiss? On the forehead? A kiss from my father couldn't have been more harmless.

HERNANI. No. It was a lover's kiss, from husband-to-be, a jealous man. Soon you'll be his. Have you thought about that? He's senile. He thinks he needs a wife to lead him to the end of the road. He doesn't see himself marrying death soon while he holds your hand. The fool throws himself between us without fear. I wish he'd see a gravedigger and show what he's made of. Who arranged this marriage, anyway?

DONA SOL. Some say the King wants it.

HERNANI. The King! My father died, condemned by his father. And though we have all aged since the day he hung, my hate, for the now dead King, and for his son, for his widow, for all his blood, is fresher than ever. My father is no longer of this world, but still, as a child, I swore to avenge his death by killing his son. I search for you everywhere, Carlos, King of the Castilles. Hate rules between our two families. My father fought for thirty years. Thirty years, only to lie dead in vain. Peace shall never come. So it is you, Carlos, who wants to violate my love. All the better. Another reason to number your days.

DONA SOL. You frighten me!

HERNANI. Now that I am banished from the kingdom, it is time that I frighten myself. The man you are to marry, your uncle, Ruy de Silva, the Duke of Pastrana, a count, and a cousin of the Castillian kings, is a very old man. His gold and jewelry will make up for his lack of youth. You will shine with the best of royalty. You may even be envied. Your rank, your pride, glory and riches may even put to shame the greatest of queens. So that, my love, is the present situation. I, Hernani, have nothing! As a child, I ran through the woods barefoot, foraging for my food. Maybe the past casts a shadow of some illustrious coat-of-arms, dulled by spilt blood or some other dishonor. While I've waited for the day that my family will rise again from the grave, the jealous heavens have yielded nothing, nothing but air, light and water... a dowry that is man's natural right. Now, you must choose between the Duke and me. One of us must deliver you. Either marry him... or you follow me.

DONA SOL. I shall follow you.

HERNANI. So you can live with me and my rude companions? Men so condemned that the executioner knows them by name? Men whose hearts and steel never dull? Men who have unavenged blood as their reason for being? Will you command them? How well do you know me? I am hunted throughout Spain. Old Catalonia, my mother, receives me alone in her forests, cliffs and summits, where only eagle can find me. I grew up with her hill people, a free and serious people, though poor in the material sense of trinkets and baubles. Tomorrow, if I were to sound my horn in their mountains, three thousand of their brave would come to my call, and you would shudder, dear. Think again. Do you want to follow me into the woods, to the mountains, roving from coast to coast with a mob of men, aware of the lot of them at all times? Their eyes, their voices, their every step... their smell? Sleeping on the grass, drinking from streams and listening to bullets whistle past while nursing our child? Is this the life you want to live? Do you want to be always on the move, hunted and banished from your land? Are you willing to follow me to my father's fate at the hands of an executioner?

DONA SOL. I will follow.

HERNANI. The old Duke is rich and prosperous. There is no stain on his father's name. He offers you treasures, titles, happiness.

DONA SOL. We'll leave tomorrow. Please, Hernani. Don't blame me for my audacity. Are you my downfall or my savior? It does not matter, I am your slave. Listen. Go where you will, I will follow. Whether you stay or leave, I am yours. Why? I only wish I knew. I need to see you again and again. I need to have you all the time. When you leave, and the sound of your step disappears into the night, my heart stops. When you leave me, I sense something missing. But, when the footsteps I long for ring in my ears, they remind me that I am alive. My soul lives again.

HERNANI. Angel!

DONA SOL. At midnight, tomorrow, bring your escort. Knock three times beneath my window. Go. I'll stay brave.

HERNANI. Now, do you know who I am? Do you realize…

DONA SOL. My lord, what does it matter? I will follow.

HERNANI. No! Since you wish to follow me, woman, you must know what name, what station in life, what soul, what destiny is hidden in Hernani, the shepherd. Do you really want a criminal? Do you want a marked man?

Enter **DON CARLOS** from the cupboard.

DON CARLOS. Are you through with your life's story? Do you think that it's comfortable in here?

11

HERNANI. (places hand on sword) Who is this man?

DONA SOL. Heavens! Help!

HERNANI. Quiet, Dona Sol! You might open some jealous eyes. When I am close, call for no one's help but mine. What are you doing here?

DON CARLOS. It is quite apparent that I am not on my Sunday stroll.

HERNANI. Who laughs after such an insult, may not live to laugh again.

DON CARLOS. To each their time. Let us be frank, sir. You love Madam and her dark eyes. Your own reflect in hers every night. That is all very well. I love Madam also. I needed to know who it was I saw at her window every night while I waited at the door.

HERNANI. For honor's sake, you may exit by my usual entrance, sir!

DON CARLOS. We shall see. I now offer my love to Madam. Better yet, let's share. I see enough love for the two of us. So tonight, I came in by surprise, hid myself, and listened, trying to keep quiet in that hole. I only managed to suffocate myself. Oh, and I wrinkled my vest, dear me… so I came out.

HERNANI. My sword is as uncomfortable as you were. It dearly wants out.

DON CARLOS. As you please, sir.

HERNANI. (drawing his sword) En garde!

DONA SOL. Hernani!

DON CARLOS. (drawing his sword) Calm yourself, Madam.

HERNANI. Tell me your name.

DON CARLOS. Your name, sir!

HERNANI. My name is for another who will one day hear it as he feels my dagger searching out his heart in his breast.

DON CARLOS. What is his name, then?

HERNANI. What does it matter now? En garde! Defend yourself!

> **HERNANI** and **DON CARLOS** cross swords. A **KNOCK** sounds at the main door.

DONA SOL. My God! Someone's knocking!

> Enter **DONA JOSEFA**.

HERNANI. Who's knocking?

DONA JOSEFA. Madam! It's the Duke!

DONA SOL. The Duke! All is lost! Oh my!

DONA JOSEFA. Oh! The unknown one decided to fight! What a scene! What a scandal!

> **HERNANI** and **DON CARLOS** sheath their swords. Another **KNOCK** sounds.

HERNANI. What can we do?

VOICE. Dona Sol! Dona Sol! Open up!

HERNANI. Don't open it.

DONA JOSEFA. St-Jacques save us!

HERNANI. Let's hide.

DON CARLOS. In the cupboard?

HERNANI. Get in. We shall survive.

DON CARLOS. Are you sure it's not too large for the both of us?

HERNANI. (motioning to the small door) Let's go this way.

DON CARLOS. Good night, then. I shall remain here.

HERNANI. Your blood shall pay for this, sir. What if I barricade the door?

DON CARLOS. Open the door.

HERNANI. What is he saying?

DON CARLOS. Let him in, I tell you!

> **KNOCK**ING continues. **DONA JOSEFA** opens the door.

DONA SOL. This is surely the end!

GOMEZ. Servants! Help me! Fetch my dagger, knife, and hatchet! You two! Follow me!

DON CARLOS. Duke, I am not here to steal your bride-to-be. I come to tell you of the death of Maximillian, the Holy Roman Emperor.

GOMEZ. What are you saying?

GOMEZ recognizes **CARLOS**.

My God! The King!

DONA SOL. The King!

HERNANI. The King of Spain!

DON CARLOS. Yes, I am Carlos. Are you mad, Duke? I was just informed that my grandfather lies dead. I came in haste to tell you myself. After all, you are a trusted, admired subject, and I need your counsel. I tried to come incognito, but all of this noise!

GOMEZ. Why was I not let in when I first knocked?

DON CARLOS. Lest you forget, Duke, you came with an armed escort! I did not travel through the night to enlighten your pages with state secrets.

GOMEZ. Your highness, forgive me, it appeared that...

DON CARLOS. Good Duke, I make you governor of Figueroa… but who will I choose to govern you?

GOMEZ. Forgive me…

DON CARLOS. Enough! Not one more word from you on the subject. The Emperor is dead.

GOMEZ. Your grandfather is dead?

DON CARLOS. Given that my grandfather was Emperor, yes, he is dead, Duke. You see me before you in the deepest of sorrows.

GOMEZ. Who is to succeed him?

DON CARLOS. A Duke of Saxony has presented himself. Francois the First of France is also in the running.

GOMEZ. Where will the Electors assemble?

DON CARLOS. I think they have chosen Aix-la-Chappelle, though they may meet in Spire, or in Frankfurt.

GOMEZ. Has our exalted king given a thought to the Empire?

DON CARLOS. I assure you, Duke, that he always has.

GOMEZ. It is almost your right, sire.

DON CARLOS. I know.

GOMEZ. Your father was Archduke of Austria, and the title held by your dearly departed grandfather, I hope, shall soon be yours.

DON CARLOS. I am also the Bourgeois of Ghent.

GOMEZ. In my youth, I saw your grandfather. Sometimes, sometimes, I wade again and again through my century. Everyone is dead now. Your grandfather was a powerful and magnificent Emperor.

DON CARLOS. Rome awaits me.

GOMEZ. He was valiant… firm in thought and deed. He was never a tyrant. His good head supported a heavy crown. It must be painful to be so young and immersed in anguish for the dead.

DON CARLOS. The Pope wants Sicily back, which I now have. An Emperor, by law, cannot hold Sicily. If he makes me Emperor I'll give him Naples, too. Once I get the eagle on my coat-of-arms, we'll see if he can clip my wings!

GOMEZ. What a joy for your grandfather to look down from the Heaven to see you on his throne, your head supporting the crown. You mourn him well, sire.

DON CARLOS. The Pope is a shrewd man, but what is Sicily? An island supported by the rest of my kingdom. A tattered rock, holding on weakly to Spain, lagging behind. "What will you do, my son?" he'll say. "With this hunchbacked island in the Empire, dragging you down? Your Empire needs to be tailored. Quick, bring me some scissors and a patch or two. We'll fix what ails you!" And I will, with good fortune. For Sicily and a few other trinkets, I'll have the Holy Empire.

GOMEZ. Console yourself, highness. Heaven is an empire of just, dead men. Your grandfather is safe.

DON CARLOS. Francois is an ambitious man. He made an eye for the Empire at my grandfather's last breath. Isn't he satisfied ruling France? France is a good piece of real estate. You'd think he has enough on his hands. My grandfather would tell King Louis of France, "If I was God the Father, and I had two sons, I would make the eldest Jesus Christ and the youngest King of France." Do you think Francois has a chance?

GOMEZ. He knows how to win.

DON CARLOS. But everything would have to change! The law excludes foreigners from the Holy Office.

GOMEZ. Are you eligible as King of Spain.

DON CARLOS. No. But as the Bourgeois of Ghent, I am.

GOMEZ. The last campaign Francois waged heighten his chances.

DON CARLOS. The eagle which may hatch on my coat-of-arms can also deploy its wings.

GOMEZ. Does your highness know Latin?

DON CARLOS. Very little.

GOMEZ. The German nobility love to be spoken to in Latin.

DON CARLOS. They can content themselves with a refined Spanish. Believe your King, Duke. When the voice is loud, it matters little in what language it speaks. I must leave now for Flanders. Your King, dear Gomez, will return an Emperor. The King of France is now scheming. I have no time to waste if I wish to take the election.

GOMEZ. You leave us lord, without purging Aragon of its bandits? They are teeming in the hills.

DON CARLOS. I've ordered the Duke of Arcos to exterminate the lot.

GOMEZ. Did you also order their chief to let himself be killed?

DON CARLOS. What? Who is this chief? What is his name?

GOMEZ. I don't know, but they say he is a rude fellow.

DON CARLOS. He'll not be too rude dead. I have it from good sources that he is in Galicia. A few of my militia should put him out of business for good.

GOMEZ. Then the news must be false that he is in the immediate area.

DON CARLOS. Yes, it must be. Tonight, Duke, you will lodge me.

GOMEZ. (bowing) Thank you, your highness! Valets! Come, make our royal guest comfortable.

DONA SOL (aside to **HERNANI**) Tomorrow at midnight. By my window. Be there. Knock three times.

HERNANI. Tomorrow then.

DON CARLOS. (aside) Tomorrow! Lady, since you must take your leave, I offer you my hand.

HERNANI. (aside) I'll offer him my dagger!

DON CARLOS. (aside) Our mystery man seems trapped. (taking **HERNANI** aside) I gave you the honor of crossing swords with me. I suspect you for a thousand reasons. But, I, King Carlos, find treason repugnant. Go. I condescend to let you escape.

GOMEZ. Who is this, lord?

DON CARLOS. He's part of my contingent. He's leaving now. Show me your fine accommodations, Duke.

ALL exit save **HERNANI**

Act I, Scene 4

HERNANI. Yes, King. I am part of your contingent. Night and day, step by step, I'll follow you, dagger in hand. My honor follows the destiny of your honor. So, now I am your rival in love. For an instant, I hesitated between loving and hating you. In loving her, I forgot my hatred, my driving force. I'm glad you've come to me. You've saved me the trouble of hunting you down. Never will a palace dog be as diligent as I in following your steps. I ask not for favors. I ask for blood. My dagger shall speak for me in due time. Go where you please, I will follow. My vengeance will guide my dagger to your heart. Without a sound, it will find its mark. May the Lord God save you.

Act II, Scene 1

Enter **DON CARLOS**, **DON SANCHO**, **DON MATIAS**, and **DON RICARDO**.

DON CARLOS. So this is the balcony and that is the door. I can hardly wait. But no light yet! Every other window is lit save the one I want.

DON SANCHO. My lord, let us talk again about this traitor. And you let him go! For shame.

DON CARLOS. As you say, Sancho.

DON MATIAS. Maybe he was the leader of the band.

DON CARLOS. Who cares? Be he leader or lackey, never have I seen anyone with such stubborn pride.

DON SANCHO. His name, my lord, what was it?

DON CARLOS. Munoz… Fernan… his name ended with an 'e' sound.

DON SANCHO. Hernani, perhaps?

DON CARLOS. Yes.

DON SANCHO. It was him, then.

DON MATIAS. Hernani? The chief!

DON SANCHO. Do you remember anything he said?

DON CARLOS. No! I couldn't hear a bloody thing inside that cupboard.

DON SANCHO. Why did you let him go when you had him?

DON CARLOS. You have a question, Count? Come aside here. Listen. I was there for another reason. I am head over heels in love with his mistress. Her eyes are dark beyond comparison. Two mirrors! Torches! Beams of sunlight in this dark world. I heard nothing but three words. "Tomorrow at midnight." That, my friend, is all. This situation is excellent. While Hernani, the bandit, wastes his time with a few random murders, I, Carlos, will steal his dove from the nest.

DON RICARDO. Your highness, it might be wiser to finish this business by first killing the vulture and then taking the dove.

DON CARLOS. Count, that is a worthwhile piece of advice.

DON RICARDO. What circumstances please the King that I should be a Count?

DON SANCHO. It's a mistake.

DON RICARDO. The King called me a Count.

DON CARLOS. Enough. I let the title drop. Pick it up.

DON RICARDO. Thank you, lord.

DON SANCHO. Surprise counts are always the quicker ones.

DON MATIAS. (aside to **SANCHO**) What will the King do once he has her?

DON SANCHO. He'll make her a Countess, and then a lady of honor. If ever a son comes out of it, he shall be King.

DON MATIAS. A bastard? King? Count, were we kings, we would still not know how to get a King out of a Countess.

DON SANCHO. Then he'll make her a Marquise, my dear Marquis. There are always ways.

DON MATIAS. Bastards rule conquered lands. They become Viceroys. That's all they are good for…

DON CARLOS. Gentlemen, wouldn't you feel safe to say that we are being observed? Finally! Those two windows are finally dark. Let's go, sirs. I wish time would go faster. Waiting seems to be my only pastime.

DON SANCHO. That is what we often say at your highness'.

DON CARLOS. My people tend to say the same when in your house. The last one is out! Light up, window. Come shine in the night, Dona Sol, a constellation against the backdrop of eternity. What time is it, Ricardo.

DON RICARDO. It will soon be midnight, lord.

DON CARLOS. We must be quick. The other one may be here at any moment. There's her shadow. The sun doesn't rise as well! Quick, give her the signal. Knock three times. You'll see her in an instant. You three get back into the shadows, you might scare her off. Let's share the two lovers when he shows up. You take the outlaw and I'll take the girl.

DON RICARDO. Thank you, lord.

DON CARLOS. If he comes, nail him to the cobblestones with your swords. While he picks up his spirits from the ground, I'll steal the belle and we can all laugh about it over some port. Don't kill him! He's brave, after all, and death is too messy in love.

Act II, Scene 2

    A **KNOCK** sounds.

DONA SOL. Is that you, Hernani?

DON CARLOS. I best keep quiet.

    Another **KNOCK** sounds.

DONA SOL. I'm coming.

    DONA SOL opens door.

Hernani!

    DONA SOL sees **DON CARLOS**
approaching.

My God, that's not his step!

DON CARLOS. Dona Sol!

DONA SOL. Oh no! That's not his voice. I'm
doomed.

DON CARLOS. Eh? What more loving voice
could you want. It is a King in love speaking.

DONA SOL. The King!

DON CARLOS. Ask me, order me, and the
kingdom is yours. I am Carlos, the King, your
love… Carlos, your slave.

DONA SOL. Help! Hernani!

    DON CARLOS grabs **DONA SOL**.

DON CARLOS. You have nothing to fear. It's not your bandit that holds you, it's your King.

DONA SOL. No! You are the bandit! Aren't you ashamed? I blush for you. Is this an exploit a King can be proud of? Does a King have to take a woman by force in the dead of the night to have her? My bandit is worth a hundred of your kind. If heaven had been fair, and given men their rank in life according to the quality of their souls, you, King, would be the thief and he would surely be King.

DON CARLOS. Madam.

DONA SOL. Have you forgotten that my father was a mere Count?

DON CARLOS. I'll make you a Duchess!

DONA SOL. Go, I would be ashamed in your shoes. There can be nothing between us, Carlos. My father spilled his blood for you. I am a noble. My rank is too low to be your wife, and too high to be your whore.

DON CARLOS. I'll make you a Princess.

DONA SOL. Send your love somewhere else, Carlos. If you dare continue to treat me like this, I can very well show you how noble I am.

DON CARLOS. Share my throne and my name! Come with me. You'll be Queen, Empress even.

DONA SOL. No. All you offer me is glitter. And besides, I would rather be outside the law and society, on the run year round, with my King, Hernani. I'd rather share his poor destiny then be an emperor's empress.

DON CARLOS. This man must be a happy one.

DONA SOL. He's as happy as any starving outlaw can be.

DON CARLOS. He does well to stay poor and banished. He is loved! I, with all my riches, am alone. An angel follows him. Do you hate me?

DONA SOL. I don't love you.

DON CARLOS. Well! It matters little whether you do or not. You'll come to me because my hand is stronger. You'll come because I want you. I am not the King of Spain and the Indies for nothing.

DONA SOL. Have mercy, my lord. What? You are the sovereign. You are King. Any Duchess, Marquise and Countess you want is yours. All you have to do is choose. The women of the court always have love for their King. But my banished one, what have the heavens given him? You have Castille, Aragon, and Navarre, and ten other kingdoms, Flanders, the Indies and their gold mines, they all bow before you. Your empire is so vast, the sun never sets on it. Why must you take me, a poor girl, from one who has nothing but me. You have everything.

DON CARLOS. Come now, I'm listening to none of this. If you come with me you'll have four of my Spains. Tell me, which ones do you want? Choose! I command you to choose, now!

DONA SOL. All I want from you is this dagger.

> **DONA SOL** grabs **DON CARLOS'** dagger.

Come one step closer, King!

DON CARLOS. You're quite charming. It comes as no surprise that you love an outlaw.

DONA SOL. One step and you die. Then I follow. Hernani! Hernani!

DON CARLOS. Be quiet!

DONA SOL. One step and it's over!

DON CARLOS. Madam! Your excess has gone too far. I have three men outside, waiting.

> Enter **HERNANI**.

HERNANI. Four, King!

Act II, Scene 3

HERNANI. And I thought I would have to trouble myself to find you. Heaven is my witness that I did not trouble myself.

DONA SOL. Save me, Hernani!

HERNANI. Quiet, love.

DON CARLOS. What are my men doing out there? Why did they let you by? Sancho!

HERNANI. Your friends are in the hands of mine. Don't bother calling for their swords. For every three of yours that come to your aid, sixty will come to mine. One chosen randomly from the sixty is worth four of yours, so let's end this quarrel here and now. What is the meaning of this? You, the lord King of Castille, try to harm this innocent girl. Your actions are reckless, not to mention lazy.

DON CARLOS. I need no reproach from you, thief!

HERNANI. He laughs! I am no king, but when a King insults and mocks me, he heightens my anger. Take care, King, for to affront me is to fear me soon after. My anger is redder than your coat-of-arms will ever be, King. You are a fool if you think you still have hope.

> **HERNANI** grabs his arm.

Do you know whose hand is on your arm? Listen. My father was put to death by yours. I hate you. You took my title and lands… I hate you! And worst of all for you, King, we love the same woman, which gives me just one more reason to hate you, body and soul.

DON CARLOS. That's all very well.

HERNANI. Yet, tonight, my hate was far away, I had but one desire and need… Dona Sol. Full of love I hurried here, only to find your disgusting person at this residence, the very person I had forgotten about tonight. You must be insane, King. You are caught in your own trap. You have no hope of escape or help. What will you do now, King? What will you do, surrounded by desperadoes?

DON CARLOS. Go ahead, start the interrogation.

HERNANI. Only one arm will have the pleasure of striking you down… mine. My vengeance dictates it! Defend yourself, King!

DON CARLOS. I am the lord, your King! Strike me down if you wish! I will not fight a duel. Kings do not duel.

HERNANI. But we dueled yesterday, King. What's wrong?

DON CARLOS. Yesterday, I didn't know your name as you were ignorant of mine. Today, friend, you know who I am and I know who you are.

HERNANI. Maybe.

DON CARLOS. I will not duel. You may assassinate me if you wish.

HERNANI. Do you really think that kings are sacred to me? Defend yourself! En garde!

DON CARLOS. You'll assassinate me first. Do you believe that you band of blood-stained marauders can hide themselves in the city? Do you think that we, the cheated victims, will condescend to knighting your daggers with our swords? No. Your crimes bog you down. You drag them with you wherever you go. Duel with you? I'd rather you stabbed me in the back! Come, kill me now and be done with it.

    HERNANI breaks his sword.

HERNANI. Get out of here. We'll meet again elsewhere. Out!

DON CARLOS. Very well, sir. But in a few hours, I, your King, will pay a visit to the local Duke. My first business on arrival will be to send for my fiscal minister. Have we put a price on your head yet?

HERNANI. Yes.

DON CARLOS. I declare you, sir, from this day, a rebel and traitor to the crown. You'll be hunted everywhere, and banished from my kingdom.

HERNANI. I've already been banished, King, a rebel and a traitor.

DON CARLOS. Excellent! My government is more efficient than I thought.

HERNANI. France is next door. France is asylum.

DON CARLOS. Soon, I'll be Holy Roman Emperor. I'll have you banished from the Empire as soon as the crown touches my head.

HERNANI. Whatever you wish, King. I have the rest of the world to brave you in.

DON CARLOS. What will you do when I have the world.

HERNANI. Then I'll have the tomb.

DON CARLOS. I'll always know how to foil your insolent plots.

HERNANI. Vengeance is sometimes like a lame old man. It comes slowly, but it always arrives at its final destination, death.

DON CARLOS. I'll hold your lady hostage.

HERNANI. Need I remind you that your life is still in my hands? Don't remind me or your imperial eagle may never hatch and die an egg.

DON CARLOS. I need no reminder.

HERNANI. Then get out of here. Leave.

> **HERNANI** takes off his coat and gives it to **DON CARLOS**.

Take this coat and wear it as you leave. Otherwise, my men might decide to let their knives slip. Leave quietly now. Your sacred egg is safe for the moment.

DON CARLOS. Never ask me for grace or mercy.

> **DON CARLOS** exits.

Act II, Scene 4

DONA SOL. Let's get out of here, now.

HERNANI. It suits you now, to be always with me in my misfortune. You want to be with me until the end of our days. A noble plan, worthy of your true heart! But it's too late for you, too late to bring joy to my cave, too late to join me in my life, too late to drag you off without shame or regret. Your beauty makes a King jealous. But it is too late. I see the scaffold in the distance, waiting for me. I have an appointment with death.

DONA SOL. What are you saying?

HERNANI. The King I braved face to face, will punish me for having dared to spare his hide. He's running to his castle now. Maybe he's already there. He calls together his guards, lackeys, lords and executioners.

DONA SOL. Let's hurry then. We'll escape together.

HERNANI. Together? No. It's too late. The hour has passed. When you revealed your love, I could only offer you my self, a miserable wretch. Along with my mountains, woods, streams, a green bed in the forest, and half of my peasant's loaf. That was fine, but I can never offer you half the scaffold. The scaffold is all mine.

DONA SOL. But you had promised me!

HERNANI. In the instant that death comes, camouflaged in the shadows, I will die the envy of all men, a happy man, for you have loved me. My death will come easy, know that I have loved and have been loved.

DONA SOL. Hernani.

HERNANI. Blessed be the soft and lucky fate which placed this flower on the edge of my abyss. It's not to you I speak but to God.

DONA SOL. Let me follow you.

HERNANI. It would be a shame to pick the flower and take it with me as I plunged into the abyss. Go! It was enough to breathe your perfume. Join the days I wrinkled in your life to the other days before and forget! Marry the old man. I release you now for I must go on into the night. Be happy and forget.

DONA SOL. No! I am yours. I want to share the scaffold. I will follow!

HERNANI. Let me go alone.

DONA SOL. You are leaving me, Hernani. Having given you my life, I have been refused, denied. I can't even have the pleasure, after so much love and pain, of dying next to him.

HERNANI. I am an outlaw! A marked man who's soon to be dead.

DONA SOL. You are an ingrate!

HERNANI. Well then! I'll stay! You want me here! Here I am. Come into my arms. I'll stay as long as you want me. We'll forget together. Here, sit here. The flames in your eyes flood my pupils. Sing me some songs like you use to, while you cried. Let's be happy and drink while the cup is still full. This hour is ours and the rest of the time is nothing. Talk to me. Ravish me. Let me sleep and dream at your breast.

    BELLS sound.

DONA SOL. Those bells! Do you hear them? Oh my! It's the alarm!

HERNANI. No. They are ringing our wedding.

DONA SOL. Get up! My God, get out now. All of Saragossa is awake.

HERNANI. We'll be wed by candlelight.

DONA SOL. It will be a wedding of the dead! It might take place in a tomb if you don't hurry!

HERNANI. Come into my arms.

    Enter a **BANDIT**.

BANDIT. My lord! The police are coming through the square. They've sent half a regiment!

DONA SOL. Ah! You were right!

BANDIT. Help, lord!

HERNANI. Don't worry. I am here.

CONFUSED CRIES. Death to the outlaw!

HERNANI. Give me your sword.

HERNANI. Goodbye, my love.

DONA SOL. This is all my fault. Where are you going? Come. Let's escape through this door.

HERNANI. What? And leave my friends? What are you saying?

More **CRIES** from outside.

DONA SOL. This noise is confusing. I'm at a loss. Remember, if you die, I die.

HERNANI. A kiss!

DONA SOL. My love! My master! My Hernani!

HERNANI. (kissing **DONA SOL**) This is the first!

DONA SOL. It might well be the last.

Exit **HERNANI** and **BANDIT**.

Act III, Scene 1

GOMEZ. Finally! Today is the day. In just an hour's time there'll be no more of this 'uncle' business. We shall be man and wife, Duke and Duchess. But have you forgiven me yet? I admit it, I was unreasonable. I reddened your forehead and paled your cheek. I suspected those two too quickly. I shouldn't have condemned you without first listening, but it seemed as if it was happening. Those two handsome young men seemed to be there for other reasons. I should have never believed my eyes, but what can you expect, child, when one is old?

DONA SOL. You always talk about that. Who can blame you?

GOMEZ. I was wrong. I should know that, with your soul, we have no other lovers on the side because we are Dona Sol, and we have in our heart good Spanish blood.

DONA SOL. Yes, my lord, my blood is good and pure. Perhaps you'll see it soon.

GOMEZ. Listen. One is not the master of his own self when he is as much in love as I am with you… as old as I am. One is jealous… mean… and why? Because one is old. Because beauty, grace, and youth in others scares us. Youth menaces. We are jealous of others and ashamed of ourselves. What a joke that this love forgot to renew my youth. When a young shepherd passes, and there are some that pass often, while we walk, him singing and me dreaming, him in his green meadow, me in my dark halls, I often say to myself that I'd give my towers and dungeon, my wheat and forests, the vast herds that mow my hills, my old name, my distinguished titles, my ruins, all my ancestors waiting for me in heaven, for his cottage and his young head. For his hair is black, and his eyes, like yours, sparkle. You can see him and think of his youth. It reminds you of how old I am. And I thought that it was enough to have Silva as a name. This is what I think while my mind wanders. Do you see how I love you? I'd give everything to be young with you, but what am I dreaming of here, me, and handsome and young? I'll be long dead by the time your turn comes.

DONA SOL. Who knows?

GOMEZ. Believe me, my love. These frivolous knights have no love for you that doesn't use itself up in words. Oh… a girl loves and believes everything heard. She laughs. All these young hawks with their painted wings and sentimental chirping, have a love that molts with their feathers. The older ones, whose age has faded all their color and voice, have surer wings, and, though less handsome, make better husbands. Old men live well. The hearth remains young and forever bleeds. My love for you is no glass toy that shines well but breaks at a touch. My love is serious, paternal, solid, sure, and friendly. My love for you is made of solid oak… a throne. That is how I love you. And I love you more still in a hundred different ways. I love you as one loves the dawn, as one loves the flowers, as one loves the heavens! To see you every day, your gracious step, your pure forehead, the beautiful fire in your eyes, is ecstasy! I laugh, for my soul is in constant celebration.

DONA SOL. Oh!

GOMEZ. The world will honor you, and it will find it just, that you, a woman, a pure angel, an innocent dove, helped me die, gave me shelter, and condescended to tolerate a useless old man who only had enough strength left to die. The work is sacred and rightly praised. It is a supreme gift to pretend to love a dying old man. You will be for me an angel with a woman's heart who brightens an old man's soul. You will be in my final years a daughter by your respect and a sister by your pity.

DONA SOL. Far from preceding me to the grave, my lord, you may follow me. Being young, itself, is no good reason to live. I've told you often that old men are always late and that young people sometimes go before them, their eyes closing quickly, like a door slammed shut by the wind.

GOMEZ. Oh! All this talk of dread! I would scold you, child, if this were not such a joyous and sacred day! Speak of which, why are you not ready for the chapel? Why are you not dressed for the occasion? The hour draws near. Quick! Go get dressed. I count the seconds. Get your wedding dress on.

DONA SOL. There will always be time enough.

GOMEZ. No. There won't be.

Enter a **PAGE**.

What is it, Iaquez?

PAGE. My lord, there's a man at the door… a pilgrim, a vagabond. In any case, what does it matter? He asks my lord, for asylum.

GOMEZ. Whoever he may be, let him come to me. Happiness enters with any stranger we receive. Is there news from the outside? What has been said about the chief of the bandits that fill our forests with rebellion?

PAGE. They say it is the work of Hernani, called by some the "Lion of the Mountain."

DONA SOL. (aside) My God!

GOMEZ. What?

PAGE. The bandits have been annihilated. The King himself, rumor has it, was chasing them down. Hernani's head is worth a thousand of the King's crowns, but some say he lies dead already.

DONA SOL. (aside) What? Without me, Hernani?

GOMEZ. Thank God the rebel is dead! We can rejoice now, my love. Get dressed now, all is well in Spain. Today, we have two reasons to celebrate.

DONA SOL. (aside) I'll wear mourning clothes.

Exit **DONA SOL**.

GOMEZ. Have this case of jewels given to her.

GOMEZ sits down.

I want to see her graced like a Madonna, beautiful enough with her eyes and jewels to make the pilgrim fall to his knees in admiration. Tell the one who asks us for shelter to enter. Ask his forgiveness for keeping him waiting. Run quickly and fetch him.

Exit the **PAGE**.

It is bad to keep one's guest waiting.

Enter **HERNANI** disguised as a pilgrim. The **DUKE** rises to greet him.

Act III, Scene 2

HERNANI. Peace be with you, my lord.

GOMEZ. Peace be with you, guest. Are you not a pilgrim?

HERNANI. Yes.

GOMEZ. Without a doubt, you must have come from Armillas.

HERNANI. No. I took another route. There's fighting going on there.

GOMEZ. The bandit's troops?

HERNANI. I have no idea. I took a different route.

GOMEZ. And the chief, Hernani, what of him? Do you know?

HERNANI. My lord, who is this, this Hernani?

GOMEZ. You don't know him? Good! The big reward won't be for you. You see, this Hernani is a traitor, a rebel to the King. He's run around long enough unpunished. If you continue your journey to Madrid, you might be there in time to see him hang.

HERNANI. I was not planning on going to Madrid.

GOMEZ. His head is for whoever wants it.

HERNANI. (aside) Let whoever wants it come and take it.

GOMEZ. Where are you going, good pilgrim?

HERNANI. I'm going to Saragossa, my lord.

GOMEZ. Oh? Did you make a vow to the honor of a saint? Of Our Lady?

HERNANI. I made a vow to the honor of Our Lady.

GOMEZ. Del Pilar?

HERNANI. Yes, Del Pilar.

GOMEZ. A man must have no soul to not follow through on his vows. Once you are finished, do you know what you'll do? To see Del Pilar, is that all you desire to do?

HERNANI. Yes. I want to see the candles and flames. I want to see Our Lady light up the end of her somber corridor with her relics and golden cape. After that, I'll return home.

GOMEZ. That is all very well. Your name, brother? I am Don Ruy Gomez de Silva.

HERNANI. My name?

GOMEZ. You can keep it to yourself, if you so wish. No one has the right to know it here. Are you not asking me for asylum?

HERNANI. Yes, Duke.

GOMEZ. Thank you. Be the welcome one, here. Stay, friend, and make yourself at home. As for your name, you shall be called my guest. It does not matter who you are, whoever you may be. I'd lodge Satan himself, if God sent him to me.

Act III, Scene 3

GOMEZ. And here is my lady. Pray to her and she will bring you much happiness.

> **DON RUY GOMEZ** presents the hand of **DONA SOL** to **HERNANI**.

Come, my beautiful bride… What? No ring? Where is your wedding ring?

HERNANI. Who wants to be a thousand crowns richer?

> **HERNANI** rips his pilgrim's robe off.

I am Hernani!

DONA SOL. Thank heavens! He's alive!

HERNANI. I am the man everyone is looking for. You wanted to know if my name was Peres, or Diego? I am called Hernani. It's a much nicer name, an outlaw's name. You see this head, Duke? It's worth more than enough to pay for your wedding. I give it all to you. You'll be well paid for this. Take me. Bind my hands and feet, tie me up. It's useless, a chain binds me from which I'll never escape.

DONA SOL. Oh!

GOMEZ. This is madness. My guest is insane!

HERNANI. Your guest is an outlaw.

DONA SOL. Don't listen to him.

HERNANI. I said what I said.

GOMEZ. Sir! A thousand crowns is a large sum, and frankly, I'm not too sure about the quality of my help.

HERNANI. What does it matter? I'll go peacefully. Take me in! Sell me!

GOMEZ. Shut up, will you? Someone might actually believe you!

HERNANI. Friends! The time is ripe! I am the outlaw, the rebel, Hernani! A thousand crowns is no laughing matter!

GOMEZ. Shut up!

HERNANI. Hernani! Right here!

DONA SOL. (aside to **HERNANI**) Shut up!

HERNANI. (to **DONA SOL**) I see someone's about to get married here. I want to be part of it, too. My bride also waits for me. (to **GOMEZ**) She's much less beautiful than yours, Duke, but I assure you, she is more faithful. Death is more faithful than any bride. (to the **VALETS**) Have any of you decided yet?

DONA SOL. Please!

HERNANI. Hernani! One thousand crowns!

GOMEZ. God must have sent me Satan.

HERNANI. (to a young **VALET**) Come! Take me, you. You'll get the money and you can start being a rich man instead of a lackey. (to the other **VALETS**) You don't want me, do you? I thought the world was against me. And now this.

GOMEZ. Brother, by touching your head, they risk losing theirs. Were you Hernani, or worth a thousand times a thousand crowns, were they to offer an empire instead of money, it would not matter. You are my guest. So being, I am bound by natural law to protect you, even against the King. It is God's will. May I die if one hair falls from your head in my house. (to **DONA SOL**) My niece, you are to be my wife in less than an hour. Go to your room and prepare yourself. I'm going to secure the castle and bolt the main door. Until then.

> Exit **DON RUY GOMEZ** followed by his **VALETS**.

HERNANI. I don't even have a knife.

> **DONA SOL** pretends to exit.

Act III, Scene 4

HERNANI. I compliment you on your dress. I can't even tell you how much the dress charms and enchants me. I love it.

HERNANI goes to the jewel box.

This ring is in good taste. Your crown more than pleases me. This gold necklace shows the finest of craftsmanship. This bracelet is also rare. And what did you do for all these? A little of your love, perhaps? You can live with your shame? These are all fake, I venture to say, fake pearls, copper instead of gold, glass and lead, false diamonds, sapphires... all fake jewelry. It's all fake, false! You are nothing but glitter Duchess! No. All of it is real, all good, and all beautiful. He wouldn't dare fool you, not with one foot in the grave. It's a shame he has everything.

HERNANI takes all the jewelry from the box.

Necklaces and earrings, a crown for the Duchess and a gold ring. Marvelous! Surely the greatest thanks for a sure, certain love, deep and faithful unto death. Such a precious little box.

DONA SOL. You didn't look to the bottom of the box.

DONA SOL takes dagger from box.

It's the dagger I took from King Carlos. He offered me a throne and I refused it, because of you, ingrate!

HERNANI falls to his knees.

HERNANI. Please, forgive me. Take my blood for your bitter tears. Only on my knees can I ask you to erase all of this.

DONA SOL. Hernani! I love you and forgive you. I have but love for you.

HERNANI. She loves me and forgives me! Who could do more than myself, after all that I said. I ask for forgiveness. She loves me. Where have you walked so I can kiss the pavement?

DONA SOL. My love!

HERNANI. No, you should hate me. Tell me that you love me. Reassure a doubting heart, tell me! For often, with three small words, has a woman's mouth healed many wounds.

DONA SOL. To think that my love has so little memory!

HERNANI. I blasphemed! If I were you, Dona Sol, I would have enough. I'd be tired of this furious idiot, this madman, who knows not how to love until he has hurt. I'd tell him, "Get lost!" Rid yourself of me while there is still time. I would bless you, for it would be right. You've supported me too long. I am evil. I've blackened your days with my nights. Enough! Your soul is noble and pure! Is it your fault if I am mean? Marry the old Duke, he's good for you. He has Olmedo by his mother and Alcala by his father. Be rich with him, be happy. What can my generous hand offer you that is as magnificent as his holdings? A dowry of pain... a choice between blood or tears. Exile, the pillory, death and all the other terrors that surround me. It would never match your gold necklace or crown. Never would a bridegroom be so proud to offer a richer box of misery and mourning! Marry the old man, I tell you. He deserves you. Do you think my outlawed head would ever go well with your crowned one? Who, when seeing us together, you, calm and beautiful, me, violent and dangerous, you, peaceful, as quiet as a shaded flower, me, blown by the storm, who could say that we deserve the same fate? No. The good Lord did not make you for me, or I for you. I have your heart, but I have stolen it. I concede it to someone more distinguished than I. Heaven never consented to our love. If I ever said that it was our destiny, I was lying to you and to myself. I'm ashamed of having been raised to hate and not having learned how to love. Forgive me and then leave me! These are my only two wishes. Carry them out, for they are my last. You will live and I shall die. I see no reason for you to rot along with me in my tomb.

DONA SOL. Ingrate!

HERNANI. I bring evil to all who come in contact with me. I took Spain's best sons, without proper remorse, and made them fight for my rights. They now lie dead, unburied. They were the most valiant of this nation. Now they are all dead, their backs on the very mountains that raised them. They would see the sky if only they could open their eyes! That is what happens to all who join me. Are you jealous of my destiny? Dona Sol, take the Duke, take Hell, take the King! All that isn't of me is worth more. I have no more friends that remember me, they're all dead! It is time for the end. I must be alone. Flee from my infection, don't make loving a religion. For your sake, get out! Don't deceive yourself! I am evil incarnate! A silent agent of mysterious origins. A bad soul forged in the fires of Hell! Where am I going? I don't know. But I feel myself being pushed to some insane end by some damn breeze. I descend and descend. I cannot stop myself. If by chance, out of breath, I dare look back, a voice tells me to press on down, and the abyss widens as I descend. I see the red flames of blood approaching as I near the bottom. Meanwhile, everything around me, everything, dies. It all falls apart. Death comes to all I touch! Flee! Get out of my way! I'll do you harm, whether I want to or not!

DONA SOL. Great God!

HERNANI. My demon is a strong one, I tell you! My happiness is the only thing that escapes him, and you are my happiness! You are not for me. Find yourself another lord and master. Go, and if Heaven smiles, don't believe a thing you see. It would all be too ironic. Marry the Duke!

DONA SOL. So, it wasn't enough, then! You've already torn my heart but now must break it! You don't love me any more!

HERNANI. You are my heart and soul. The home of all my strength is you! You don't want to flee, you want to be loved.

DONA SOL. I have nothing against you, my lord. I was dying for your love.

HERNANI. Dying? For who? For me? How can one die for so little?

DONA SOL. (bursting into tears) I can say no more…

HERNANI. You're crying! You're crying and it's all my fault, again. Who will punish me? You'll just forgive me, again. Who can tell you what I suffer when tears drown the fire in your eyes, my joy? My friends are dead and I am going insane! Forgive me. I would like to love, but I know not how. I seem to love. Don't cry. Let's die instead! If I had a world, I would give it to you! Happiness has never followed my step.

DONA SOL. You are my lion! I love you!

HERNANI. Love would be God's gift to man if we could die from too much of it.

DONA SOL. I love you, my lord. I have nothing but love for you.

HERNANI. A dagger from you would be soft!

DONA SOL. Don't you think that God punishes you when you speak like that?

HERNANI. Well, let Him take us apart, then. You want it this way, so let it be. I resisted for as long as I could.

> **DONA SOL** and **HERNANI** embrace.
> **DON RUY GOMEZ** enters, unnoticed
> by the two lovers.

Act III, Scene 5

GOMEZ. So this is how you repay me for my hospitality?

DONA SOL. My God! The Duke!

GOMEZ. Is this what I deserve, guest? Go see if the walls are being guarded, if the door is well bolted and if my archer is in his tower. Go see if someone is making the rounds for your sake. I even looked for armor that would fit. Try to put on your battle armor when you're sixty! So this is your loyalty! This is what you do for us after all we have done for you? Lord! I've lived long and I thought I had seen it all! I've often erected the executioner's scaffold on my very doorstep for lawless bandits, assassins, counterfeiters, traitors, valets who had poisoned their masters. I've seen some die without the cross and absolution. I saw Sforce, I saw Borgia and now I see Luther, but I've never seen such perversity! Betraying your host invites lightning to strike you down. All this is not of my time. This treason petrifies me, an old man, in my very house. I'll look ready for the grave before my time! Moors and Castillians! Who is this… man? Oh you, all the Silvas that can hear me now, forgive me if my anger makes me forget the virtue of hospitality!

      HERNANI stands up.

HERNANI. Duke…

GOMEZ. Shut up! Sacred dead! Elders! Men of
steel! You've seen what came from Heaven and
what came to this world from Hell. Tell me, lords,
tell me, who is this man? He's not Hernani, he's
Judas! Speak so I may hear his name!

> **DON RUY GOMEZ** crosses his arms
> and waits for the portraits on the wall to
> speak.

Did you ever see anything of the kind in your day?
No!

HERNANI. My lord Duke…

GOMEZ. (addressing the portraits) Do you see
this? The ingrate wishes to speak! You can read
his soul better than I. Don't listen to him, he's a
cheat. He sees some vengeance hatching in the
storm of my heart. He'll tell you that he's an
outlaw. He'll tell you that they'll be saying Silva as
they would say any other name, and that he is my
guest as well as yours. My forefathers, my lords,
do you see? Is it my fault? Judge us!

HERNANI. Ruy Gomez de Silva. If ever noble
eyes have looked to the sky, if there ever was a
heart so big, a man so distinguished, it is you, sir!
It is yours, my host! I, who talk to you here, am
guilty. I have nothing to say, save that I am already
doomed, condemned. Yes, I wanted to take your
bride from you. Yes, I wanted to soil your bed. I

must be insane, it must be my blood, the blood you have every right to spill. You'd do well to do it now, to wipe your sword clean and forget about it.

DONA SOL. My lord! It's not his fault! Strike me down if anyone must fall!

HERNANI. Your tongue, Dona Sol! This hour is supreme, for it is mine. It is all I have left, so let me explain myself to the Duke. Duke, as my last wish, believe me, I swear, I am the guilty one. Kill me, but spare her, for she is pure. That is all. I am guilty and she is pure. Give her your faith and give me the sword or dagger. Throw my corpse out on your porch for the dogs. Have the floor washed for the wedding.

DONA SOL. No! I did it all myself! I love him! Forgive me! I love him, lord!

GOMEZ. You love him? Tremble then, sir!

Enter **PAGE**. **NOISE** from outside.

What's all this noise?

PAGE. It is the King, my lord, in person with a platoon of archers. His herald knocks.

DONA SOL. My God! The King! What else can happen now?

PAGE. He asks why the doors are bolted shut. He wishes to enter.

GOMEZ. By all means, let him in.

PAGE bows and exits.

DONA SOL. All is lost!

> **DON RUY GOMEZ** goes to his own portrait and turns a secret knob. A door opens. He motions to **HERNANI**.

GOMEZ. Enter here, sir.

HERNANI. My head is yours. Deliver it, sir. I hold it ready for the executioner. I am your prisoner.

> **HERNANI** exits out secret door.

DONA SOL. My lord! Have mercy!

PAGE. His Highness, the King!

> **ALL** bow. The **KING** and **CONTINGENT** enter.

Act III, Scene 6

DON CARLOS. I never thought to see the day, cousin, when your door is so well secured. And I thought your dagger was rusty! I didn't know you had it ready in hand to shine in our eyes when we came to visit.

> **DON RUY GOMEZ** makes an attempt to talk. **DON CARLOS** stops him.

You are trying to be a young man rather late in life, no? Do you now wear a turban? Why don't you call me Abu or Mohammed instead of Carlos? Answer me! What causes you to lower the grill and raise the drawbridge?

GOMEZ. Lord…

DON CARLOS. Secure the keys. Guard the door and let no one out.

> Two of **DON CARLOS' OFFICERS** exit.

So you've decided to resurrect a long-dead rebellion, Silva? By God man! If you take these airs with me, Duke, the King will be a King! I'll go to the mountains and kill them all with my own calloused hands in their very nests!

GOMEZ. Lord, the Silvas are loyal…

DON CARLOS. Don't stall, Duke. Answer me or I'll raze your eleven towers! From the extinguished blaze there remains one spark. From the dead bandits there remains one chief. Who's hiding him? Are you? I suspect that this scum, this Hernani, is in your castle. You are hiding him!

GOMEZ. My lord, it's true. I am hiding him.

DON CARLOS. Excellent, my good man! I want his head, cousin, or yours. Do you understand?

GOMEZ. Then mine will fall, sir, and you will be satisfied.

>**DONA SOL** falls to the floor.

DON CARLOS. That's an improvement! Now, fetch me my prisoner.

>**DON RUY GOMEZ** crosses his arms and lets his head fall. **DONA SOL** and **DON CARLOS** remain silent. **DON RUY GOMEZ** takes **DON CARLOS'** hand and leads him to the portraits on the wall.

GOMEZ. This one was the first of the Silvas, Don Silvius. He was a great man, three times consul to Rome.

>**DON RUY GOMEZ** passes to the next portrait.

Here is Don Galceran de Silva, the other Cid! He is buried at Tora where a hundred candles burn on his golden sepulcher. He delivered Leon from the tribute of one hundred virgins.

> **DON RUY GOMEZ** passes to the next.

Don Blas, who, of his own will and good faith, exiled himself for having given his King bad counsel.

> Passes to the next.

This is Christoval. At the battle of Escalona, the King fled on foot, wearing a white feather in his cap. Christoval took the feather and gave the King his steed.

> To the next.

Don Jorge, who paid the ransom of the King of Aragon, Ramirez.

DON CARLOS. By God, Don Ruy! I truly admire you and your dead. Now, my prisoner!

GOMEZ. (moving to the next portrait) Here is another Ruy Gomez de Silva, Grand Knight of the orders of St. Jacques and of Calatrava. His giant armor would never fit us. He took three hundred flags, won thirty battles and conquered for his King Matril, Antequera, Suez, and Nifar. He died a poor man. Salute him, my lord.

> **DON RUY GOMEZ** pauses and then moves to the next portrait.

Near him, his son, Gil, dear to loyal souls. His hand was as trustworthy as any royal one when it came to taking oaths.

> Passes to the next.

Don Gaspar of Mendoza and Silva. All the noble houses must deal with the house of Silva in one way or another. Sandoval has always feared or married us. Manriquez envies us and the Laras are jealous of us. Alancranste hates us. We touch all of them, even the kings.

DON CARLOS. Are you railing?

GOMEZ. (passing to the next) There is Don Vasquez, the wise, and Don Juan, the strong. One day, the two stopped Zamat and over one hundred Moors, by themselves... and I have passed over some of the better ones, lord.

      Passes to the next.

And this is my grandfather. For sixty years, he kept the faith.

      Passes to the one before the last.

This old man, this holy man, is my father. He was great, even if he was the last. The Moors made his friend, Alvar Giron, a prisoner. So my father carved a statue of Alvar in stone. He dragged it with him, swearing by his patron saint that he would never retreat. The stone Count and six hundred men of war did not look back once. My father fought, found the Count, and saved him.

DON CARLOS. My prisoner!

GOMEZ. He was a Gomez of Silva. What you have just heard are the stories we tell in this house whenever we visit these heroes.

DON CARLOS. My prisoner on the hour!

GOMEZ. (leading **DON CARLOS** to the last portrait) This last portrait is of me. Thank you, King Carlos, for you want people to say when they see it, "This last one, the dignified son of a race of noble men was a traitor, having sold the head of his guest."

DON CARLOS. Duke, your castle hampers me. I'll raze it to the ground.

GOMEZ. You'll pay me well for his head, won't you?

DON CARLOS. Duke, your castle shall be razed for such audacity. Hemp shall grow in its place!

GOMEZ. It is better to see hemp grow where my towers once stood than to see the name of Silva stained.

DON CARLOS. Duke, his head is ours. You had promised me...

GOMEZ. I promised you one or the other. (to the portraits) Is this not true? I give you my head. Take it!

DON CARLOS. Very well, Duke, but I don't like losing out! The head I want, the head I need, is young. Once dead, I must have it by the hair. With your head, I'll lose out. The executioner will try to hold on in vain, you don't have enough hair to fill his hand.

GOMEZ. Spare the affrontment, your Highness. My head is still well preserved, and is surely worth as much, I think, as the head of a rebel. I think it is an insult that the head of a Silva is not sufficient for you.

DON CARLOS. Give me Hernani.

GOMEZ. Truly, I did say…

DON CARLOS. Search everywhere! Let there be no wing, no cave, no tower…

GOMEZ. My dungeon is as loyal as I am. Only it knows my secret and we will forever share it between us.

DON CARLOS. But I am the King!

GOMEZ. Outside of you making the stones of my demolished castle my grave, you shall have nothing!

DON CARLOS. It appears that my begging and menacing are all in vain. Get me the bandit, Duke, or I'll have your head and your castle. I'll slaughter everything.

GOMEZ. I have spoken.

DON CARLOS. Very well, I'll have two heads instead of one. Jorge, place the Duke under arrest.

DONA SOL. You are a bad King, Carlos!

DON CARLOS. Great God! Dona Sol!

DONA SOL. Your Highness does not have the heart of a true Spaniard!

DON CARLOS. Madam, you are very severe towards your King. It is you who puts this anger in my heart. A man either becomes an angel or a demon by touching you. When we are hated we quickly become mean. If you had wanted it, little girl, I'd be great. I'd be the Lion of Castille! Instead, you made me a tiger with your anger. Watch him roar, Madam, and hold your tongue.

> **DONA SOL** looks angrily at **DON CARLOS**. **DON CARLOS** bows.

DON CARLOS. I'd obey you, though. My cousin, you have my esteem. Your scruples, after all, seem legitimate. Be loyal to your host and disloyal to your King. It's all very well. I forgive you and in so doing am better than you. Only one thing… I'm taking your niece hostage.

GOMEZ. Only one thing!

DONA SOL. Me, my lord?

DON CARLOS. Yes. You!

GOMEZ. No more? Is that all? What clemency! Oh, generous victor, you save the head and torture the heart. What kindness!

DON CARLOS. Choose quickly, Duke, Give me Dona Sol or the traitor. One or the other.

GOMEZ. You are the master!

> **DON CARLOS** approaches **DONA SOL** to take her away. **DONA SOL** runs to **DON RUY GOMEZ**.

DONA SOL. Save me, my lord! Wretch, you must go with one or the other. It is either your uncle's head or the other's! I must go with him! (to **DON CARLOS**) Go! I follow!

DON CARLOS. (aside) By the saints! It worked! We'll have to soften up my soon-to-be queen.

> **DONA SOL** goes to the jewelry box and takes a dagger, which she conceals in her cleavage. **DON CARLOS** comes to **DONA SOL** and takes her hand.

DON CARLOS. (to **DONA SOL**) What do we have here?

DONA SOL. Nothing.

DON CARLOS. A precious jewel, is it?

DONA SOL. Yes.

DON CARLOS. Let me see it.

DONA SOL. You'll se it.

GOMEZ. Dona Sol! Heaven and earth! Dona Sol! Crumble, armors and murals, for the men here have no guts!

> **DON RUY GOMEZ** runs to **DON CARLOS**.

Leave me my child! I have nothing but her, my King!

DON CARLOS. Give me my prisoner, then, Duke!

GOMEZ. (to the portraits) Have mercy on me!

> **DON RUY GOMEZ** walks to the hiding place.

Hide yourselves! Your faces stop me! (to **DON CARLOS**) You want him?

DON CARLOS. Yes!

DONA SOL. My God!

GOMEZ. No!

> **DON RUY GOMEZ** throws himself at the mercy of **DON CARLOS**.

Have mercy! Take my head!

DON CARLOS. Your niece!

GOMEZ. Take her then, but leave me my honor.

DON CARLOS. Good day, then, Duke. May God keep you!

> **ALL** exit save **DON RUY GOMEZ**.

GOMEZ. King, while you leave happy from my house, my old loyalty leaves my crying heart.

Act III, Scene 7

> **DON RUY GOMEZ** opens secret door.

GOMEZ. Come out.

> **HERNANI** enters through door. **DON RUY GOMEZ** shows him two swords that lie on the table.

Choose. Don Carlos has left. I must now restore my honor with arms. Choose, and choose quickly. Your hand is trembling! Choose!

HERNANI. A duel! We can't fight, old man!

GOMEZ. Why? Are you scared? Are you not noble? Hell! Noble or not to cross steel with steel, every man that outrages me is enough of a gentleman to fight.

HERNANI. Old man...

GOMEZ. Come kill me or come die, young man.

HERNANI. To die, yes. You saved me against my wishes. My life is yours. Take it.

GOMEZ. (to the portraits) Do you wish it to be? You see that he wants it. (to **HERNANI**) Very well. Say your prayers.

HERNANI. It's to you, my lord, that I address my last one.

GOMEZ. Talk about it to the other Lord.

HERNANI. No. I address it to you, old man. Strike me down! Anything will suit me, a dagger, a sword, even a knife. Just let me, out of pity, let me have one supreme joy. Duke, before I die, let me see her!

GOMEZ. See her!

HERNANI. At least permit me to hear her voice one last time! Just one last time!

GOMEZ. Hear her!

HERNANI. Oh, I understand your jealousy, my lord. But, my youth now seized by death, forgive me. Do you want me to, tell me, without seeing her, hear her? I'll die tonight. To hear her only! Satisfy my last wish! I'll take my last breath softly if you would condescend to let my soul see her's in her eyes before fleeing to heaven. I'll tell her nothing. You'll be there, old man. You can kill me afterwards.

GOMEZ. Saints in Heaven! Is the hiding place so deep, so quiet, so lost that he didn't hear anything?

HERNANI. I heard nothing.

GOMEZ. I had to deliver you or Dona Sol.

HERNANI. Deliver? Deliver to whom?

GOMEZ. To the King.

HERNANI. Idiot! He loves her!

GOMEZ. He loves her?

HERNANI. He's our rival in love. He's kidnapped her!

GOMEZ. Shit! My vassals! To the horses! To the horses! Let's get the kidnapper!

HERNANI. Listen. Vengeance on foot makes much less noise. You own my life. You can always kill me at your leisure. Do you want to have me avenge your niece and her virtue? Let me do my part. Let me, if I have to kiss your feet for permission. Let's both follow the King. Come, I'll be your arm. I'll avenge you, Duke. When all is done, you may kill me.

GOMEZ. So, I can kill you if I choose? At any time?

HERNANI. Yes, Duke.

GOMEZ. On what do you swear?

HERNANI. I swear on my father's head.

GOMEZ. Would you like to remind yourself of this someday?

HERNANI. Listen. Take this horn. Whatever happens, old man, wherever the place, whenever the hour, if it so happens that it is time that I die, come… sound the horn and worry no more, everything shall be done and over with.

> **DON RUY GOMEZ** gives **HERNANI** his hand and looks up at the portraits.

GOMEZ. Be witnesses to this…

Act IV, Scene 1

DON RICARDO. This is the place.

DON CARLOS. This is where the conspirators assemble, Charlemagne's tomb. I have them under my thumb here. The kind Elector from Treves has loaned me this place. It's well-chosen. I can hear them sharpening their stilettos on the tombstones. They're putting all their heads in one basket, though. Their heads are at stake. We'll see, by God, my dead assassins! They did well to choose a grave for this business. They won't have far to go once dead. Do these caves go far underground Ricardo?

DON RICARDO. Back to the castle, sire.

DON CARLOS. That's more than enough room to bury the lost.

DON RICARDO. Other caves, on the other side, go all the way to the Altenheim monastery.

DON CARLOS. Where Rudolph exterminated Lothaire, good. Tell me again, Count, the names and their grievances. I want to know who, how and why.

DON RICARDO. Gotha.

DON CARLOS. I know why the brave Duke conspires. He wants a German from Germany to be Emperor.

DON RICARDO. Hohenburg.

DON CARLOS. I think Hohenburg would rather have Hell with Francois than Heaven with me.

DON RICARDO. Don Gil Tellez Giron.

DON CARLOS. Jesus Lord! He's revolting against his own King.

DON RICARDO. They say that he found you at his wife's side the night you came to make him a Baron. He wants to avenge the honor of his tender companion.

DON CARLOS. So he revolts against Spain, then. Who else is there?

DON RICARDO. I noticed that the Reverend Vasquez, the Bishop of Avila, was with them.

DON CARLOS. Is he also avenging the virtue of his woman?

DON RICARDO. There is also Guzman de Lara, a peer who wants the collar of your order.

DON CARLOS. Ah! Guzman de Lara! If it's just the collar he wants, he'll get it.

DON RICARDO. And then there's the duke of Lutzelburg. As for what he wants from us…

DON CARLOS. The Duke of Lutzelburg's head is too big.

DON RICARDO. Juan de Haro wants Astorga.

DON CARLOS. These Haros always double the executioner's fee.

DON RICARDO. That is all, sire.

DON CARLOS. That's not all, Count. Count them… that only accounts for seven of them.

DON RICARDO. Ah! I didn't tell you about the bandits hired by either Treves or France.

DON CARLOS. Men without prejudices or qualms. Their daggers are always ready, ready to turn to the most money offered, like magnets to a pole.

DON RICARDO. I saw two of them, both new arrivals, an old man and a young one.

DON CARLOS. Their names?

> **DON RICARDO** shrugs.

Their age?

DON RICARDO. The younger cannot be more than twenty.

DON CARLOS. That's too bad.

DON RICARDO. The old one is surely over sixty.

DON CARLOS. One's not quite old enough and the other is over the hill. Oh well, I'll take care of them. The executioner can count on my good credit. My sword is not dull when it comes to taking care of these various factions. I'd readily loan it to him if his own sword was dulled. If, Count, the scaffold needed widening, I'd loan him my imperial robe to sew onto it. But shall I ever be Emperor?

DON RICARDO. The electoral college is deliberating at this hour.

DON CARLOS. What can I ever be certain and sure of? They'll name Francois the First or their Saxon, their Frederick the Sage. Ah! Luther has good reason. Everything is running so badly! And to think that they are the ones who make us sacred! They only accept reason in the form of money. A heretic Saxon! A Palatine Count who's an imbecile! A primate from Treves who's a degenerate. As for the King of Bohemia, he is mine. The Princes of Hesse are smaller than their province! You idiots! Perverse old men! So what if they have crowns? They're dwarves sitting on a ridiculous council that I could carry away like Hercules. Without their purple coats, they would end up with less a head than Triboulet, Francois' jester. I'm missing three votes, Ricardo! I'm missing everything! I'll give Gand, Toledo, and Salamanca, my dear friend Ricardo, three towns of their choice for three votes. Do you see, I'd give them three cities of my Flanders or Castille for their three votes. Of course, I'd eventually take them back.

DON RICARDO salutes **DON CARLOS** and puts his hat on.

Why are you covering yourself?

DON RICARDO. Sir, you referred to me in the familiar. I am now a Grandee of Spain.

DON CARLOS. (aside) Ah! I have only pity for you, you stupid ambitious! What a lot! They follow their thinking through our actions. The lower court is where the King, begged without shame, gives some crumb of greatness to his starving people! Only God and the Emperor are great... and the Holy Father! The others, the Kings and Dukes, what are they?

DON RICARDO. I, myself, hope they'll elect my Highness.

DON CARLOS. Highness? Me... Highness? I must have misfortune in all. If I remain a simple King I'll...

DON RICARDO. (aside) Enough! Whether he becomes Emperor or not, I am still a Grandee.

DON CARLOS. How will they announce the election of the new Emperor once he is chosen?

DON RICARDO. If it's the Duke of Saxony, one cannon shot. Two if it's the Frenchman. Three if it is your Highness.

DON CARLOS. And what about Dona Sol? As if I didn't have any problems! It's irritating, Count, if by chance, I am made Emperor, run and get her. Perhaps she will love me as a Caesar.

DON RICARDO. Your Highness is too kind!

DON CARLOS. Silence! I haven't yet said what I will want to think. Don't second guess me. When will I know who is elected?

DON RICARDO. In an hour, I believe, at the latest.

DON CARLOS. Three votes, that is all I need. Nothing but three. Anyway, while we are here, let's snuff the hopes of these conspiring bandits. After that, we'll see who owns the Empire.

   DON CARLOS counts on his fingers.

Always three votes shy! It's all in their hands now. This Cornelius Agrippa knows a lot, though. He saw thirteen stars in the northern sky, rushing toward my star at full speed. I will have the Empire. But, on the other hand, it is sad that Jean Tritheme, an abbot, predicted to Francois that I should have, to solidify the prediction even more, aided the prophecy with a few pieces of artillery. All predictions from the most refined sorcerers come quicker to term when a good army, cannon, pics, infantry, cavalry, bands, and music are ready to show fortune its path. They use these as midwives to deliver their predictions true. Which of the two is worth more his salt, Jean Tritheme, or Cornelius Agrippa? The one who uses an army to explain his system, who puts a bayonet at the end of what he says, the one who commissions soldiers, mercenaries, and bandits to help imperfect predictions along with their swords, tailoring events to the word of the prophet. Those who, with a proud eye and a foolish forehead, look straight into the Empire's eye and say; "I have my right to it", are very poor fools. They have many cannon, all in long file. Their red breath can melt cities. They have ships, soldiers, and horses, and you believe that they will march to the goal over the people they have crushed. Enough! At the great crossroads of human fortune, which lead more of us into the abyss than to the throne, they can barely make three steps. Undecided, uncertain, they hesitate, unsure of themselves. In doubt, they go to the nearest fortune teller to find out where they are going. (to **DON RICARDO**) Go! This is the hour that the conspirators will be here. Ah! Give me the key to Charlemagne's tomb.

DON RICARDO. My lord, you should think of the Count of Limburger, the guardian of these chambers. He gave these to me and he is at your service.

DON CARLOS. Go! Do everything I told you to do! Everything!

DON RICARDO. I go now, your highness.

DON CARLOS. Three shots, correct?

Exit **DON RICARDO**.

Act IV, Scene 2

DON CARLOS. Charlemagne, forgive me. These halls should only be filled with spare words. My ambition's babblings seem indignant to your monument, to you.

Charlemagne is here! How, tomb, can you hold this great spirit without bursting?

Are you well here, giant? Can you truly sleep here, despite your size? It's an extravaganza fit to ravish the senses, to see, how Europe is now, and how it was when you left it.

Europe is now a great building, with two men at the top, two chiefs to whom all born King must submit themselves. Almost all of the states, duchies, military fiefs, kingdoms, and lands are now hereditary. But the people, once in a while, have a Pope or Caesar they call their own.

Life goes on, destiny corrects luck. From all of this emerges an equilibrium and ever-changing order. Two sacred senates, the Electors with their golden capes, and the Cardinals in scarlet, strike the world dumb.

But they only parade briefly. God wants what He wants. If an idea, suited to the needs of the time, is hatched, it grows quickly, mixing with everything. It becomes human, seizes hearts, and digs a furrow into the soil, entrenching itself.

Many a King, with the crowds teeming at his feet, gags on this idea. But if it enters some morning into the Diet or Conclave, all kings will suddenly be slaves to this idea.

This idea shall tread on their heads, whether it wears the tiara or carries the imperial globe. The Pope and Emperor are everything. Nothing is on this earth that is not there for them or because of them. They have all the earthly rights to the mystery that lies between themselves and Heaven. Heaven keeps them under it's cloud where the thunder roars.

The two sit alone at God's table. There, He serves them the world. Face to face they sit, managing, regulating, arranging the universe as a farmer might arrange his fields. All is done through these two. Kings wait at their door, sniffing the odd vapor of meals brought to the two, peering through the window on their tiptoes, attentive and very lonely.

The world falls into place beneath them and regroups. The two create and destroy at will. One absolves sin, the other cuts and hacks. One is truth, the other force. They have their reasons in themselves and are, simply because they are.

When they retire from the table, both equals, the dazzled universe contemplates the whole scene in terror, the one in his imperial purple, the other in his paschal white, these two halves of God, the Pope and the Emperor!

The Emperor... the Emperor... to be Emperor! To not be and to feel one's heart full of courage! The one who sleeps here in his tomb is happy. He is great now and in his time he was greater. The Pope and the Emperor! They no longer were simply two men. Peter and Caesar! In them were coupled two Romes, fertilizing both Romes in a mystical womb, regiving the cities form, a soul to humanity, fusing whole tribes of people, and, here and there, kingdoms. All to forge a new Europe, the two using their very hands to create something with the bronze left behind by the ancient Romans.

Oh! What a destiny! Yet... this tomb is now yours all the same. Is it all worthless? Is this where we end up? What then? To be a Prince, King, and Emperor... a giant... Germany was but your pedestal! What? For a title Caesar and for a name Charlemagne? Having been greater than Hannibal and Attilla... having been as great as the world and everything that came with it and to end up here?

Intrigue then the Empire and see the dust that makes an Emperor! Cover the entire world with your noise... erect and build your Empire. Never say "It's enough!" Fashion an immense edifice with the thickest of walls. Do you know what will be left one day? The stone and not much else. Do you know what happens to the titles and the triumphant names? At best, they become a series of letters that we make the children spell. Regardless of your high goals and proud aspirations... that is all that becomes of it.

Oh... the Empire... the Empire! What does it matter to me? I touch it and find it simply to my liking. Something tells me: "You'll have it... you'll have it." If I had it! Heavens on high! To be what starts it all! Alone, standing at the highest point of an immense spiral of states, piled one on top of the other. To be the keystone of an arch and to see beneath yourself the kings, the feudal houses, the counts, the cardinals, doges, dukes, bishops, clan chieftains, and high barons! The soldiers and the clergy and far below you, in the shadows, at the very bottom of the abyss... common man.

Men? That's to say an immense sea, a huge noise, tears and cries... and sometimes a bitter laugh, a complaint that, waking the earth, frightens it. Men! Cities! Towers! A vast swarm that rings the alarm from the steeples.

The base of nations carried on their shoulders, an enormous pyramid supported at the two poles... living currents that constantly embrace it by its folds. They balance it precariously... because of the large, constant tremor. They make everyone change places, and, in the higher echelons, use the thrones as one might use a stepladder and shake them so well that all kings, ceasing their vain debates, raise their eyes and prayers to the sky, when they should be looking beneath them.

The people are an ocean. Shadows, forever turbulent, where one can't throw down anything without causing some great stir. They're a wave that pounds on the throne and lulls the tomb. A mirror in which a king rarely sees himself handsome.

If we ever looked, once in a while, down into the somber current, we'd see empires at the bottom… great vessels that have sunk, that the ocean's ebb and flow have rolled… empires that hampered it and that it no longer cares or knows about.

To govern all that! To climb, if they name you, to this, to climb, know that one is only human! To have this abyss then. That is, if the Electors don't write a different ending to this affair.

The summit is very narrow. Bad luck to the one without sure footing. Who would I hold on to if I was to fall while feeling the earth quake beneath me? What will I do once the globe is in my hands? To be Emperor, my God! I had enough to deal with being King! Only a mortal not of common stock can enlarge his soul along with his fortune… but me? Who will make me great? Who will be my law? Who will give me counsel?

DON CARLOS falls to knees.

You're the one, Charlemagne! Because God, for whom all obstacles efface themselves, takes our two majesties and places them face to face... pour into my heart, from the dregs of your tomb, something great, sublime, and good.

Let me see all of it! Show me that the world is small... for I dare not touch it. Show me that on this Babel, which, from shepherd to Caesar, goes climbing up into the sky, everyone, in their own small way, pleases and admires himself by seeing someone below them, trying hard to keep from laughing. Teach me how to reign and vanquish. Tell me it's worth more to punish than it is to pardon. Isn't it so?

Legend has it that a shadow rises, once in a great while, from his bed. It opens this large tomb and throws out a lightning bolt.

If this is true, Emperor of Germany, tell me what one can do in the steps of Charlemagne! Speak! By speaking your sovereign breath can break this bronze door in two over my head.

Or rather, let me go into your sanctuary. Let me enter to see your face and do not stop me with the north wind. Prop yourself up on your stone bed... let's discuss things. Dare you tell me, with your fatal voice, about those things that somber the eyes and pale the forehead? Talk, and don't blind your frightened son, for your tomb is certainly filled with light. If you decide to say nothing, let

Carlos study your head… let him measure you at his leisure… oh giant… for nothing here is as great as the void you left. May his ashes counsel me if his ghost can't!

DON CARLOS brings key to door.

Let us enter.

DON CARLOS steps back.

My God! If he were to speak to me! If he were there, standing and slowly pacing the tomb! Or if I came out, my hair white! I'll go in anyway.

FOOTSTEPS approach.

Someone's coming. Who would dare disturb this great dead's grave at this hour… outside of myself? Who?

FOOTSTEPS come closer.

Ah! I forgot… my assassins! I'll enter.

> DON CARLOS enters tomb.
> CONSPIRATORS enter.

Act IV, Scene 3

FIRST CONSPIRATOR. Ad Augusta.

SECOND CONSPIRATOR. Per Augusta.

FIRST CONSPIRATOR. The saints protect us.

THIRD CONSPIRATOR. The dead serve us.

FIRST CONSPIRATOR. God keeps us.

There is a **NOISE** in the shadows.

SECOND CONSPIRATOR. Who goes there?

VOICE. Ad Augusta.

SECOND CONSPIRATOR. Per Augusta.

Enter new **CONSPIRATORS**.

FIRST CONSPIRATOR. Look! Someone else is coming!

THIRD CONSPIRATOR. Who goes there?

VOICE. Ad Augusta.

ALL shake hands.

FIRST CONSPIRATOR. Good, we are all here. Friends, the shadow awaits the light. Gotha, report.

ALL seat themselves in semi-circle. **FIRST CONSPIRATOR** goes around lighting **OTHERS'** candles. **FIRST**

CONSPIRATOR then seats himself in middle.

GOTHA. Friends, Carlos of Spain, a stranger by his mother, pretends to have a right to the Holy Empire.

FIRST CONSPIRATOR. He'll have the tomb.

GOTHA. (throwing down his torch and stamping it out) I hope this happens to his head!

ALL. Yeah!

FIRST CONSPIRATOR. Death to him!

GOTHA. Kill him!

ALL. Burn him!

DON JUAN DE HARO. His father is German!

DUKE OF LUTZELBURG. His mother's Spanish!

GOTHA. He's neither German nor Spanish! Let him die!

A CONSPIRATOR. What if the Electors name him Emperor this minute?

FIRST CONSPIRATOR. Them? Him? Never!

DON GIL TELLEZ GIRON. What does it matter? Kill the head and the crown is dead.

FIRST CONSPIRATOR. If he gets the Holy Empire, he becomes, no matter what he is, holy, and then only God can lay a finger on him.

GOTHA. The best thing to do is to kill him before he becomes Emperor.

FIRST CONSPIRATOR. He won't be elected!

ALL. He won't get the Empire!

FIRST CONSPIRATOR. How many arms do we need to send him to the grave?

ALL. Only one!

FIRST CONSPIRATOR. How many knife wounds does it take to the heart?

ALL. Only one!

FIRST CONSPIRATOR. The victim is a traitor. They make an Emperor, and we take on a sacred duty. We'll draw names to pick the assassin.

> **ALL** write their names on pieces of paper and place them in an urn held by the **FIRST CONSPIRATOR**.

May the elected believe in God, strike like a Roman, and die like a Hebrew! He must brave the wheel, this man. May he sing to the wooden horse and laugh at the fire beneath him. In the end, he must kill and die a resigned man. He must do all!

> **FIRST CONSPIRATOR** picks a piece of paper from the urn.

ALL. Who is the chosen one?

FIRST CONSPIRATOR. Hernani!

HERNANI. I won! I have you now! You who I've follow for so long! Vengeance is mine!

GOMEZ. No! Let me do it!

HERNANI. No! On my life! Never! Don't take this good luck away from me, Lord! This is the first time anything good has ever happened to me!

GOMEZ. You have nothing! I'll give you everything, fiefs, castles, a hundred thousand peasants in my three hundred villages! If you just let me drive the fatal blow, friend!

HERNANI. No!

GOTHA. Your hand will give him a shallow wound, old man.

GOMEZ. If I don't have an arm, I surely have a soul! Don't judge any blade by the rust on the scabbard! (to **HERNANI**) You belong to me!

HERNANI. My life to you, yours to me.

GOMEZ. Very well, friend. Take this horn.

HERNANI. What? You give me back my life? Life means nothing to me! I'd rather have vengeance! With God's help, I know what to do in these matters. I have my father to avenge, and perhaps even more than simply that! Her... Don Sol? Do you yield her to me?

GOMEZ. Never! Take back your horn, instead.

HERNANI. No.

GOMEZ. Think about it, child.

HERNANI. Duke, cede me my prey. He is mine.

GOMEZ. Very well. Damn you for taking away the joy.

FIRST CONSPIRATOR. Brother, it would be well to do him in tonight, before he is elected.

HERNANI. Fear nothing. I know how to send a man to his grave.

FIRST CONSPIRATOR. Let all his treason come back to him! May God be with you! Let us continue, Counts and Barons, if he should die without killing him. Let us swear to strike in turn without fleeing. Carlos must die.

ALL. (unsheathing their swords) Let us swear on it!

GOTHA. (to the **FIRST CONSPIRATOR**) What shall we swear on, brother?

GOMEZ. (presenting a cross) Let us swear on this cross!

ALL. (lifting their swords) Let him die without confession!

> A distant SHOT. **ALL** are silent. Another SHOT, and then another. **DON CARLOS** enters from Charlemagne's tomb.

Act IV, Scene 4

DON CARLOS. Sirs! Go no further! The Emperor hears you!

> All candles go out.

Much silence and a deep night! The swarm comes out and then retreats into hiding. Do you really believe, gentlemen, that all this will pass away like a dream and that I pass you off, since you no longer have your candles, for stone men, sitting on their tombs? You spoke quite loud a minute ago, my statues. Let's go, now! Off with your heads, for here is Charles the Fifth! Strike me, take one step! Will you even dare? No, you will not. Your torches bloodied the cave a few moments ago. Is my breath strong enough to extinguish them all? Now, now, let us see. Turn your eyes to me, for, if I put out many, I light even more.

> **DON CARLOS** knocks his key on brass door of Charlemagne's tomb. The cave fills with **SOLDIERS** led by **DON RICARDO**.

Hurry, my falcons! I've the nest and the prey! I light the place up in my time. The grave is lit now, look! Come, all of you, for the crime is flagrant.

HERNANI. At the right hour! Alone, he seemed great. That's very well, for a moment, I thought it was Charlemagne, but it's only Charles the Fifth.

DON CARLOS. (to the **DUKE OF ALCALA**) Officer of Spain! (to the **MARQUIS OF ALMUNAN**) Here, Admiral of Castille! Disarm them!

DON RICARDO. Your Majesty!

DON CARLOS. I make you high magistrate of the court.

DON RICARDO. Two Electors come to compliment your Majesty in the name of the Assembly.

DON CARLOS. Let them enter. (aside to **DON RICARDO**) Get Dona Sol.

> Enter **KING OF BOHEMIA, DUKE OF BAVARIA** and their contingents.

DUKE OF BAVARIA. Charles! King of the Romans, your very sacred Majesty… Emperor! In your hands rests the world, for you now have the Empire. This throne that all the monarchs aspire to is yours. Frederick, the Duke of Saxony, was first elected. But, judging you the more worthy, he did not want the crown. Come, then, and receive the crown and the globe. The Holy Empire, King, makes you very great. You are revered by those of the robe and those armed with the sword.

DON CARLOS. I'll thank the College when I enter. Go, sirs, and thank you, my Bohemian brother and my Bavarian cousin. Go. I'll go myself and accept the globe and crown.

KING OF BOHEMIA. Charles, our ancestors addressed each other as friends. My father liked yours, and their fathers admired each other. Charles, you so young on the mound of contrary fortunes, tell me, do you want me as a brother amongst brothers? I saw you as a child and can never forget…

DON CARLOS. Very well, King of Bohemia. You are family.

> **DON CARLOS** presents his hand to **KING OF BOHEMIA** and **DUKE OF BAVARIA**. They kiss his hand.

Go!

> Exit **DUKE OF BAVARIA** and **KING OF BOHEMIA** with their contingents.

CROWD. Long live Carlos!

DON CARLOS. (aside) I am, now that all has passed, Emperor! All because Frederick refused the honor!

> Enter **DONA SOL** dragged in by **DON RICARDO**.

DONA SOL. Soldiers! The Emperor! Heavens! How so unexpected! Hernani!

HERNANI. Dona Sol!

> **DONA SOL** runs to **HERNANI**. He stops her with his look.

HERNANI. Madam!

DONA SOL. I always have my dagger!

HERNANI. My love!

DON CARLOS. Silence! All of you! (to the **CONSPIRATORS**) Have your souls hardened? I must give the world a lesson. Lara the Castillian and Gotha the Saxon, all of you! What were you doing here? Speak!

HERNANI. Sire, the whole matter is rather quite simple. We were merely engraving the writing on the wall.

      HERNANI draws his dagger.

We are rendering unto Caesar what is Caesar's.

DON CARLOS. Very well! (to **DON RUY GOMEZ**) You are a traitor!

GOMEZ. Which of us is the traitor?

HERNANI. Our heads and the Empire! He has what he desires! The blue coat of simple royalty might have hindered your path. The Imperial purple suits you better. Blood will not stain it.

DON CARLOS. Silva, my cousin, it's a felony to betray your nobility. It's high treason, Don Ruy. Think about that.

GOMEZ. Men without honor are fought without honor.

DON CARLOS. (to **DUKE OF ALCALA**)
Don't take away any of them who might be
Counts or Dukes. As for the others…

> The **NOBILITY** is separated from the
> **OTHER CONSPIRATORS**, who are
> placed under heavy guard. **HERNANI** is
> placed among the **OTHER**
> **CONSPIRATORS**.

DONA SOL. He's saved!

HERNANI. (emerging from the **OTHER
CONSPIRATORS**) I'll pretend that I am among
them! Since we are dealing with the axe here, and
that Hernani, an obscure shepherd, shall pass
between your legs unpunished because he is not a
noble, and, because, to die, one must be great, I
am standing up for my rights. God, who gave you
the scepter, made me Duke of Segorba, and Duke
of Cardonna, Marquis of Monroy, Count of
Alvareta, Viscount of Gor, and lord of so many
places that I forget the names. I am Juan of
Aragon, the grand master of Avis, born in exile,
the banished son of an assassinated father, killed
by your father, King Carlos of Castille! This
murder is an affair between our families. You have
the scaffold, we have the dagger. So, Heaven
made me a duke. Exile made me a man of the
mountains, an outlaw. But, because I fruitlessly
sharpened my sword on the mountains and in the
waters of Spain's strong torrents…

HERNANI puts on his hat.

HERNANI. (to the **CONSPIRATORS**) Let us cover ourselves Grandees of Spain! Yes, King, our heads have the right to fall covered in front of you! Silva, Haro, Lara! Gentlemen of title and blood, make room for Juan of Aragon! Dukes and Counts, my place! I am Juan of Aragon, King, executioners and valets, and if your scaffolds are too small, enlarge them!

DONA SOL. Heavens!

DON CARLOS. In effect, I had forgotten about this incident.

HERNANI. He who bleeds has a better memory. The affrontment that the offender forgets lives on in the heart of the offended.

DON CARLOS. Then I am, I hold a title that does not make one want to hold anymore, the son of a father who took the head of yours.

DONA SOL. (throwing herself at **DON CARLOS**) Sire, forgive! Mercy! Sire, forgive and forget, or strike both of us down for he is my lover. In him only do I breathe! Oh! Sire, have the mercy to kill us together! Majesty! I drag myself to your sacred knees! I love him! He's as mine as the Empire is yours! Forgive! Forget! What sinister plan is in your mind?

DON CARLOS. Let's go! Up with you Duchess of Segorba, Countess of Alvareta, Marquise of

Monroy… (to **HERNANI**) Have I left any out, Don Juan?

HERNANI. Who speaks like this? The King?

DON CARLOS. No… the Emperor.

DONA SOL. Great God!

DON CARLOS. Duke, here is your bride.

HERNANI. Just God!

DON CARLOS. My cousin, your nobility is jealous, I know. But Aragon can marry Silva.

GOMEZ. It is not of my nobility.

HERNANI. My hate leaves me.

> **HERNANI** throws down his dagger.

GOMEZ. (aside) Will I burst now? Oh, no! Foolish love is a fool's pain! Burn without a flame, old man. Love and suffer in secret. Let your heart gnash itself, but not one tear, for they would laugh.

DONA SOL. My Duke!

HERNANI. I have nothing but love for you!

DONA SOL. Finally! Happiness!

DON CARLOS. (aside) Extinguish yourself, young heart, full of flame! Let your spirit reign. It has troubled you a long time. Your loves and mistresses are, from now on, Germany, Flanders and Spain. The Emperor is the same as the eagle. Instead of a heart, he has but a coat-of-arms.

HERNANI. Ah! You are Caesar.

DON CARLOS. Your heart is well-deserving, Don Juan, of your nobility. You are also deserving of her. To your knees, Duke!

> **HERNANI** kneels. **DON CARLOS** takes his collar and gives it to **HERNANI**.

Receive this collar.

> **DON CARLOS** unsheathes his sword and strikes him softly three times on the shoulder.

By St. Steven, Duke, I make you knight. Be loyal.

> **HERNANI** stands and they embrace.

But you have her, the best and softest of collars, the one that I don't have, who is dearly missed at the highest of ranks. The two arms of a loved woman who loves you! You will be happy! I, I will be Emperor. (to the **CONSPIRATORS**) I no longer know your names. Hate, furor, I wish to forget them all. It was not in vain that, Charles the First, King, was succeeded by Charles the Fifth, Emperor, the Catholic Emperor in sacred majesty, and the one law changes in the eyes of Europe, the little orphaned girl in tears.

> **CONSPIRATORS** kneel.

CONSPIRATORS. Glory to Carlos!

GOMEZ. I'm the only one left who's condemned.

DON CARLOS. And what of me?

GOMEZ. (aside) But, unlike Carlos, I never gave my pardon.

HERNANI. Who then changes things so?

ALL. Long live Germany! Honor to Charles the Fifth!

DON CARLOS. Honor to Charlemagne! Leave us alone, the two of us!

    ALL exit.

Act IV, Scene 5

DON CARLOS. Are you satisfied? Did I rid myself well of the miseries of a king, Charlemagne? Am I now another man? Can I now place my helmet with those of Rome? Do I now have the right to the fortunes of the world? Do I now have sure footing that can march on this road, filled with Vandal ruins, the road blazed by your large sandals? Did I light my candle from your flame? Did I understand the voice that came to me from within the tomb?

Ah! I was alone, lost... alone in front of an Empire. A whole world screaming, menacing, and conspiring. The Dane to punish, the Holy Father to pay... Venice, Suliman, Luther, Francois of France... there are a thousand jealous daggers that glint in the shadows... traps, perils... enemies who number... twenty people of whom one alone would scare twenty kings... always hurried, everything in need of hurry and everything to do at once... I called to you asking: "How do I start?"

And you answered, saying, "My son, by clemency..."

Act V, Scene 1

GARCI. Long live joy and the bride!

MATIAS. All of Saragossa is here tonight.

GARCI. With good reason. I've yet to see a softer night, a happier night for a wedding. And never a better pair.

MATIAS. We have a good Emperor.

SANCHO. Marquis, certain nights, we would go out with him, looking for adventure until dawn. Who would have known that it would end this way?

RICARDO. I saw it all. Listen, three men, one a bandit with a noose waiting for him, the other an old duke, and the last a king, try to capture the heart of one woman. Who has her when the dust clears? The outlaw.

FRANCISCO. The story's not as simple as that. The end result of love and fortune, here in Spain and elsewhere, are always determined by loaded dice. The thief always wins.

RICARDO. I, myself, made my fortune as a voyeur. I saw love made. First, I was simply a count, and then a grandee, and finally, the leader of the palace guard. I made good use of my time.

SANCHO. The secret, sir, is to travel the king's road. Dog his step.

RICARDO. It gave value to my rights, my actions.

GARCI. You profited with all the distractions.

MATIAS. What has happened to the old duke? Is he having his coffin fitted?

SANCHO. Don't laugh, marquis! The old man has a proud soul. And he loved Dona Sol. Sixty years it took to make his hair turn gray. One night made them white.

GARCI. They say he hasn't been back in Saragossa since the Emperor's election.

SANCHO. Do you expect him to show up?

FRANCISCO. And what is the Emperor doing?

SANCHO. The Emperor is troubled. Luther saddens him.

RICARDO. That Luther! I'd finish him off quickly given four policemen.

MATIAS. Suliman also bothers him.

GARCI. Who can care about the world now? Women this beautiful are rare these days. Enjoy.

SANCHO. The gist.

RICARDO. Garci has a point. Myself, I am never the same when on holiday. It must be these masks. They give everyone a truly different identity.

SANCHO. (aside to **MATIAS**) Why can't he always be on holiday?

FRANCISCO. Isn't this the newlyweds' room?

GARCI. We'll see them in a second.

FRANCISCO. Do you really think so?

GARCI. Think so? I'm certain!

FRANCISCO. Good! The bride is so beautiful!

RICARDO. The Emperor is good… too good. This rebel, this Hernani, he has the gold collar. He's married and pardoned. If the Emperor had heeded my advice, he would have given him a bed of rocks to lie on and given the lady a bed of feathers.

SANCHO. (aside to **MATIAS**) I'd happily slip my knife into him. He's a false lord and wears a lot of useless frill.

RICARDO. Excuse me, what did you say?

MATIAS. (aside to **SANCHO**) No quarrels here, Count! (to **RICARDO**) He's singing me a sonnet Petrarque wrote to his lady.

GARCI. Have you noticed, gentlemen, amid all the good cheer and pageant, that specter, standing against the rail, staining this celebration with his black domino mask?

RICARDO. Yes, by God!

GARCI. Who is it?

RICARDO. His air and build look like Don Fresno's, general of the Marines.

FRANCISCO. No, it's not him.

GARCI. He hasn't dropped his mask one night.

FRANCISCO. He didn't have a guard. It's just the Duke of Soma, who wants to be noticed.

RICARDO. No. I just spoke with the good duke tonight.

GARCI. Who is it, then? Look. There he goes.

SANCHO. If the dead walk, that is how.

GARCI. (to the **DOMINO**) Nice mask. (to **ALL**) Lords, I saw fire in his eyes.

SANCHO. If he be the devil, he'll find me to answer to! (to the **DOMINO**) Have you come here from Hell?

DOMINO. I come not from there, I go.

Exit **DOMINO**.

MATIAS. His voice is deadly.

GARCI. Enough! He can go elsewhere and scare others. We came to the ball to laugh.

SANCHO. It must be some practical joker.

GARCI. Even if he is Lucifer come up from Hell, lets dance.

SANCHO. It must be a joke.

MATIAS. We'll know tomorrow.

SANCHO. Go out and see where he's going.

MATIAS. He's gone down the stairs. I can't see him anymore.

SANCHO. This is almost too bizarre to be a joke.

GARCI. (to the **MARQUISE**) Shall we dance?

MARQUISE. My dear Count, you know that my husband counts all of our dances?

GARCI. Which gives us all the more reason to dance. Apparently, our dances amuse him. It keeps him occupied. He counts and we dance.

Exit **MARQUISE** and **GARCI** dancing.

SANCHO. This is strange indeed.

MATIAS. Silence! Here are the newlyweds.

Act V, Scene 2

HERNANI. Dear friends!

RICARDO. Your happiness is our joy, Excellency!

FRANCISCO. My lord, Venus leads him!

MATIAS. It is honorable to be happy on a day like this night.

FRANCISCO. (showing the conjugal chamber to **MATIAS**) Great things will go on in there! To be a flea and to be there once the fires are out and the door is closed.

SANCHO. It's getting late. We should leave, should we not?

      ALL salute and exit, one by one.

HERNANI. May God keep you!

SANCHO. Be happy!

      Exit **SANCHO**.

Act V, Scene 3

DONA SOL. Finally, they've all left.

HERNANI. Dear love!

DONA SOL. It's… ah… it's very late… it seems that…

HERNANI. Angel! It's always late when we're alone together.

DONA SOL. All the noise was tedious, tiring. Isn't it so, dear lord, that all this joy dizzies happiness.

HERNANI. You speak the truth. Happiness, my love, is serious. It wants bronze hearts and engraves them slowly. Pleasure frightens happiness by throwing it flowers. Its smile is closer to tears than to laughter.

DONA SOL. In your eyes, the smile is the day.

> **HERNANI** tries to take **DONA SOL** across the threshold.

In a little while, my lord.

HERNANI. Make me wait then. Whatever you wish, I am your slave. Tell the volcano to strangle its flames. Its fissures will close, and flowers and green grass will teem its slopes, for I am taken. Vesuvius is now your slave.

DONA SOL. You are good for my soul Hernani of my heart.

HERNANI. What is this name, Madam, 'Hernani'? Call me no longer by that name. You now make me remember what I had hoped to forget. I know that there existed, a long time ago, in a dream, a man of the mountains and the night, an exile, an Hernani, whose eyes were imbedded by the lightning of the sword. An Hernani on whom the word 'branded' was inscribed. An Hernani, a wretch who rode with bad luck. But, I no longer know this Hernani. I love the meadows, the flowers, the woods, the song of the nightingale… for I am John of Aragon, Dona Sol's husband, and I am happy!

DONA SOL. I am happy, too.

HERNANI. Does it matter what rags I left at the door when I entered? Let me have what the past has given me, my courtyard, my towers, my dungeons and bastilles, my feathers and my seat on the council of Castilles. Leave us alone, the rest is now history. I saw nothing, said nothing, and did nothing. Now, I erase everything in my past and start over.

DONA SOL. This collar goes well with black velvet.

HERNANI. You saw the King place it.

DONA SOL. I never noticed it before now. All others, what do they matter? And is this velvet or satin still? The collar does not make the man. It's the neck the collar sits on, my lord. You are noble and proud, not the collar.

HERNANI starts to take her away.

Soon! Soon! Can't you see I'm crying with joy? Come, see the beautiful night. My Duke, nothing but a moment. Enough time to look and breathe. All have put out their lights, the torches and the music are now far away. There is nothing here but us and the night. It's all perfect. Tell me, do you believe that nature stays up late to watch us sleep? Nothing here… not a cloud in the sky, all rests. A few minutes ago, the moon was rising on the horizon. As you spoke, it's trembling light and your voice reached into my heart. I felt joy and calm soothe me, my love. It would have been a good time to die.

HERNANI. Who can forget anything spoken by this celestial voice? Your words are a song. Like the traveler, on a river, sliding through the waters on a soft summer's night, my thoughts dragged and erred in your song.

DONA SOL. This silence is too empty, this calm too deep. Tell me, wouldn't you like to see one star tonight?

HERNANI. Fickle woman. Just a minute ago you were complaining of the noise and the light.

112

DONA SOL. That was the ball. I want to hear a bird sing in a far off field. A lost nightingale in the shadows and moss. Or a few flutes lost in the night. Music is soft. The soul becomes harmonious. A thousand voices sing in the heart! Music would be charming now.

A **HORN** sounds in the distance.

DONA SOL. Dear God! You answered my prayers!

HERNANI. (aside) Oh, no…

DONA SOL. An angel read my mind. It must have been your guardian angel.

HERNANI. Yes, you're right, my guardian angel.

The **HORN** sounds again.

DONA SOL. Don Juan, I remember the sound of your horn.

HERNANI. Is it mine?

DONA SOL. Of course, is this a joke?

HERNANI. You said it.

DONA SOL. What a dull ball that was! I love the sound of your horn when the sound comes from the woods. Your horn is your voice.

HERNANI. (aside) The old tiger is here. He wants his prey.

DONA SOL. What's wrong?

113

HERNANI. The old man.

DONA SOL. My God! Why are you so pale? What's wrong with you?

HERNANI. The old man. He's out there, laughing in the shadows. Don't you see him?

DONA SOL. What old man? Where is he? Are you losing your mind?

HERNANI. The old man.

DONA SOL. Please. On my knees, I beg you. Tell me, what secret tears you apart? What's wrong?

HERNANI. I swore to him!

DONA SOL. You swore?

HERNANI. (aside) What could I say? I must spare her of this. Myself, I am nothing. What did I just say? What am I babbling?

DONA SOL. You said…

HERNANI. No. No, my spirit was troubled. I suffer from something, you see? Don't let it shock you.

DONA SOL. Do you need anything?

The **HORN** sounds again.

HERNANI. (aside) He wants me! He wants me now! He has my word. I have no sword. I have nothing. It must be. What must . . . must.

DONA SOL. Tell me. What troubles you so?

HERNANI. An old wound. An old wound I thought had long healed, is causing me some pain. Dona Sol, my love, listen. The small box I carried with me in the happier days...

DONA SOL. I know which one, my love. What do you want from inside it?

HERNANI. There's a vial for pain, an elixir, that can put an end to this pain.

> **DONA SOL** exits.

Act V, Scene 4

DOMINO enters.

DOMINO. "Whatever happens, old man, wherever the place, whenever the hour, if it so happens that it is time that I die, come… sound the horn and worry no more, everything shall be done and over."

HERNANI. It's him!

DOMINO. I've come to your house, and I say to you, the hour has come. Your time is here and you are late, my friend.

HERNANI. Very well. What shall be your pleasure? What will you do with me? Speak.

DOMINO. I leave the choice to you. Will it be steel, or poison. Whichever you need, I shall supply. We shall leave together.

HERNANI. So be it.

DOMINO. Shall we pray beforehand?

HERNANI. What does it matter now? Prayer is for the living.

DOMINO. Which have you chosen?

HERNANI. The poison.

DOMINO. Good. Your hand, sir. Good. Drink so that I may end it also.

DOMINO hands **HERNANI** vial.

HERNANI. Let me live this tomorrow. If you still have a heart, Duke, a conscience, if you are not a ghost out of Hell, a condemned corpse, a phantom, a demon, you will never do this. If you know what love is. To be twenty years old and to love, to marry your loved while you can still love, if ever a woman trembled in your arms, wait until tomorrow. Tomorrow, come tomorrow.

DOMINO. You must be naïve. Tomorrow? You mock me. Your bell tolled this morning. And what will I do tonight? I am dying. If I die, who will come to get you? I will not go to the grave alone. Follow me, young man, you must.

HERNANI. No. From you, devil, I deliver myself. I won't obey.

DOMINO. I suspected you might not. Very well. By the way, what did you swear upon? You swore upon nothing, obviously. Very little… the head of your father. A father's memory can be always forgotten. Youth is fickle.

HERNANI. My father! My father! I must have been losing my mind!

DOMINO. No. You perjured, betraying yourself and your family.

HERNANI. Duke!

DOMINO. Since the oldest Spanish house plays games with their words, good night, boy.

HERNANI. Don't leave.

DOMINO. What then? Do I stay and watch you live?

HERNANI. You are cruel, old man, but I will follow your steps to Peter's gate.

Enter **DONA SOL**.

Act V, Scene 5

DONA SOL. I couldn't find your box.

HERNANI. (aside) It's her! What a time for her to walk in.

DONA SOL. What is it? I scare him. He seems to stagger at the sound of my voice. What is that in your hand? Answer me! What's that in your hand?

    DOMINO unmasks himself.

It's poison!

HERNANI. Great God!

DONA SOL. What did I do to you? What was it? You're cheating on me, Don Juan.

HERNANI. I should have said nothing! I promised the Duke that saved me that I would die at his wish. Aragon must pay his debt to Silva.

DONA SOL. You're not his to have. You're mine. What do all your other oaths matter to me? Duke, love makes me strong. Against you and all others, I will defend him.

GOMEZ. Defend him if you can, against a sword oath, nothing human.

DONA SOL. What oath?

HERNANI. I swore to it.

DONA SOL. No. Nothing holds you to it. This can't be. It's a crime, an insane crime.

GOMEZ. On with it.

HERNANI. Leave me be, Dona Sol. It must be this way. The duke has my word and my father watches from on high.

DONA SOL. You'd have better luck trying to steal a cub from a tiger's lair. Do you know what it is to be Dona Sol? For a long time, out of sheer pity for your age, what I might have thought to be respect for your age, I played shyly, timid and innocent. But, you see me now, humid eyes teared in rage.

> **DONA SOL** takes dagger from her dress.

DONA SOL. Do you see this, old man? En garde, Don Ruy. I am of your family, but terror to the one who puts one hand on my husband.

> **DONA SOL** throws dagger aside.

Ah! I fall to my knees! Have mercy! Mercy my lord, I am but a woman! I am weak, sapped of force, my soul dies before you! I beg you, on my knees, have mercy!

GOMEZ. Dona Sol!

DONA SOL. Forgive me, but we, the Spanish, tend to place our pain in words, you know that.

You are not evil incarnate. Have mercy, Uncle. Kill one of us, we both die. Mercy! I love him!

HERNANI. You're crying!

DONA SOL. No! I don't want you to die! I don't want it to happen. No, give us your grace! I would love you well also, Duke.

GOMEZ. After him! From these scraps of love… of friendship… less even. Do you think you could quench the thirst which devours me? He is alone. He is all. But myself… pity! What can I do with your friendship? You would be giving me alms from his kingdom. You would be serving me the dregs of your love. No. We must be done with it. Drink.

HERNANI. He has my word. I must be true to it.

GOMEZ. Now. On with it!

DONA SOL. Not yet! Listen to me, both of you!

GOMEZ. The crypt is ready. It will wait no longer.

DONA SOL. One instant, my lord, my Don Juan! Both of you are cruel. What do I want from you but one second? That is all, all I want. Let a poor woman say what she has in her heart. Let me speak.

GOMEZ. I'm getting anxious.

DONA SOL. My lords, you make me tremble! What did I ever do to deserve this?

HERNANI. Ah! Her tears tear me apart!

GOMEZ. It is time to die.

DONA SOL. Don Juan, after I am through, all that you want to do, you can.

> **DONA SOL** takes the vial from **HERNANI**.

I've got it!

GOMEZ. I seem to be dealing with two women. I'll go find two brave souls elsewhere, Don Juan. You make easy oaths on the blood that made you. I'll speak with your father about it tonight, once I've joined the dead. Good night!

HERNANI. Duke, stop! I beg you, do you want me to be false, a liar? Do you want me to travel the rest of my life, treason tattooed on my forehead. Please, the poison. Give it to me. For our souls' sake, for love's sake.

DONA SOL. Do you want some?

> **DONA SOL** drinks from the vial.

Here, take it.

GOMEZ. Ah! She took it from him for herself!

DONA SOL. Take it, I tell you!

HERNANI. Do you now see, old man?

DONA SOL. Don't worry about me. I took your part of the poison.

HERNANI. My God!

DONA SOL. You wouldn't have left me enough, you! You, you don't have a Christian bride's heart, do you? You don't love like a Silva. But, I was the first to drink and I am still quiet. Go! Drink if you want?

HERNANI. What did you do?

DONA SOL. You wanted it.

HERNANI. It's not a kind death.

DONA SOL. No? Why's that?

HERNANI. It carries you with fire to the tomb.

DONA SOL. Weren't we sleeping together tonight, anyway? What does it matter in what bed we sleep?

HERNANI. My father, avenge thyself on your son who has forgotten his and your name.

DONA SOL. My God! What pain! Get rid of it! Throw it away! I've lost all reason! Stop! The poison is strong, Don Juan, strong… it hatches a hydra that gnaws at the heart. I didn't realize what anguish one suffered, so close to death. It's fire, don't drink it! You'll suffer too much!

HERNANI. Your soul is cruel, old man. Couldn't you have chosen another poison for her?

HERNANI drinks and tosses the vial aside.

DONA SOL. What are you doing?

HERNANI. What did you do?

DONA SOL. Come, come my love... into my arms. Isn't this a horrible death?

HERNANI. No.

DONA SOL. Our wedding night begins. I'm very pale, it seems, for a bride.

HERNANI. Oh!

GOMEZ. The deed is done.

HERNANI. It's hopeless. To see my bride suffer... to watch her die.

DONA SOL. Calm yourself. I am better now. To newer lights... we shall unfurl our sails. Let's have a good journey to a better world. A kiss... only a kiss...

GOMEZ. This is painful.

HERNANI. Blessed be Heaven that gave me such a life... full of pitfalls... haunted by ghosts of a time past. Blessed be Heaven that permits me... after a long trek... to die, my lips on your hand.

GOMEZ. Look how happy they are.